The Principles of Islamic Marketing

This book is dedicated to my mother, Khadra, and to my father, Ahmad, with love and appreciation.

The Principles of Islamic Marketing

BAKER AHMAD ALSERHAN
United Arab Emirates University, UAE

GOWER

Published by
Gower Publishing Limited
Wey Court East
Union Road
Farnham
Surrey, GU9 7PT
England

Ashgate Publishing Company
Suite 420
101 Cherry Street
Burlington,
VT 05401-4405
USA

www.gowerpublishing.com

British Library Cataloguing in Publication Data
Alserhan, Baker Ahmad.
The principles of Islamic marketing.
  1. Marketing--Islamic countries.
  I. Title
  658.8'0091767-dc22

  ISBN: 978-0-566-08922-0 (hbk)
  ISBN: 978-1-4094-2894-7 (ebk)

Library of Congress Cataloging-in-Publication Data
Alserhan, Baker Ahmad.
The principles of Islamic marketing / Baker Ahmad Alserhan.
    p. cm.
  Includes index.
  ISBN 978-0-566-08922-0 (hardback) -- ISBN 978-1-4094-2894-7
  (ebook) 1. Markets--Islamic countries. 2. Islamic countries--Commerce. I. Title.
  HF5475.I74A47 2011
  658.80088'297--dc22
                                                                    2010052247

Printed and bound in Great Britain by the MPG Books Group, UK

Contents

List of Figures

List of Tables

Preface

Beyond worship, the duty of people in Islam is to build *Emaar* (the earth). The exact meaning of the Arabic term *Emaaratu Alardh* (building of the earth) means to make it full of life or, to make it better in every sense. A term intrinsically related to *Emaar* is *Ifsad* (ruination). The Islamic teachings state that the duty of man is to build without causing ruination before, during or after the building. If cutting a tree to make pencils – the greatest invention of mankind – leads to soil erosion then cutting that tree becomes classified as ruination to the earth and as such it becomes forbidden. A pencil manufacturer, thus, needs to think of more innovative and less harmful ways to make pencils.

Islam takes a very long-term perspective in determining what is permissible (*Halal*) and what is not permissible (*Haram*). Making gains today at a deferred price that earth and its inhabitants will have to pay later is *Haram*. The religious aim of trade in Islam, like all other human activities, is to make the world better. Thus, all those involved in trade must ensure, each in his turn, that a tree is planted in place of the tree that they need to cut down, that adequate and safe passage ways are allowed for animals when designing dual carriage ways, that planting coffee to increase the wealth of one doesn't mean planting less wheat making another starve, etc.

These and other similar concepts are not hard to comprehend and they don't conflict with human nature; it is easy for people to know that harm in all of its forms and shapes is wrong, but the Islamic doctrine doesn't stop at clarifying right from wrong or good from bad; instead, it makes it obligatory on its followers and all those who deal with them to adhere to its teachings of causing no harm. Failure to comply with these teachings, when one is able to comply, becomes a sin.

Islam is a framework of life and living. It is much more than *Halal* or *Haram*, permissible or not permissible, right or wrong or, good or bad. The duty of man on this earth is to enable life to thrive; cutting down a forest to erect concrete, high rise or otherwise, is neither building nor enablement! I still remember a story a Portuguese friend told me many years ago that when a tree was cut down in the Amazon, scientists found nearly four thousand species and life forms living off and on that tree. It is within this framework that the Islamic teachings on business should be understood; before carrying out any business activity, a business person needs to make sure that he can justify the displacement of four thousand lives. If no justification can be provided then the tree should be left alone.

About this Book

In the global corporate environment today there are very few books that provide practical perspectives and insights relating to the Islamic viewpoint on business conduct, ethics and other managerial issues. *Principles of Islamic Marketing* addresses one aspect of Islamic business thought that has been thus far neglected; it aims to provide a framework for understanding the Islamic marketing code of conduct and presents practical perspectives for companies and their leaders and employees to incorporate.

This is not a religious book and it is addressed neither to new age Muslims nor to traditional Muslims. It is written as a marketing book that aims at filling a gap in international business literature, that which represents the basis of the business model adopted by nearly one quarter of the world population: the Islamic economic system. This model has already proved successful in one major industry: Islamic finance. Although a thriving financial sector sounds unrealistic these days, Islamic finance, as a branch of the Islamic economic system, is one sector that has not only been resilient, but it is also growing faster than any other subset of world banking. While the Western world's financial system has been imploding, this small but rapidly growing share of world capital has emerged relatively unharmed. Many Western banks, trying to cash in on this growing field, have fast-growing Shariah-compliant arms. The UK is vying to capture this market and has changed its laws to allow the different property transfers required for Islamic lending. British media report growing interest even among non-Muslims because of perceptions that it is a more ethical approach to finance.

The book provides a complete guide of the requirements an organization needs to follow when managing its entire marketing function within the Muslim market or when a Muslim part is involved. Being the first publication in this field, it is designed not only to address the challenges facing marketers involved in business activities with and within Islamic communities, the knowledge needs of academic institutions or the interest of multinationals keen on tapping the massive Islamic markets, it aims, above all, to lay the foundation of and advance Islamic marketing as a new social science. Furthermore, it identifies the features of the Islamic framework of international marketing practices and ethics in the sense that marketing practices, embedded in a strong ethical doctrine, can raise the standards of business conduct without compromising the quality of services or products offered to customers, or harming the interests of businesses. Adherence to such ethical practices elevates the standards of behaviour of traders and consumers alike (Saeed et al. 2001), creates a value-loaded framework for firms and establishes harmony and meaningful cooperation between international marketers and their Muslim target markets.

Throughout the book, I have used the following Quran translations:

1. Yusufali, available at The Center for Muslim–Jewish Engagement, University of Southern California

2. Pickthal, available at The Center for Muslim–Jewish Engagement, University of Southern California

3. Shakir, available at The Center for Muslim–Jewish Engagement, University of Southern California

4. available at http://www.qurancomplex.com/Default.asp?l=eng#.

References

Saeed, Mohammad, Zafar U. Ahmed and Syeda-Masooda Mukhtar (2001). 'International marketing ethics from an Islamic perspective: a value-maximization approach.' *Journal of Business Ethics* 32 (2): 127–42.

PART 1

Understanding Islamic Marketing

Islamic Business Ideals

When Muslim merchants travelled to distant lands, the inhabitants of those lands were impressed by the traders' social and business conduct and so became curious about their beliefs. Many of these inhabitants subsequently became Muslims.

Rice, 1999

Learning Objectives

After reading this chapter, you should be able to understand:

- The Islamic law, Shariah
- The three categories of Muslims' practices and acts
- The four sources of the Islamic ethical system
- The principles governing Islamic ethics
- Islamic values in business
- Implications for business.

Introduction

In an era when there is an increased and renewed emphasis on teaching and learning business ethics, the highly pertinent question being raised is the role of faith and religious beliefs on business practices. Do religious beliefs help produce more ethical organizations and consumers? As a major world religion with clearly defined rules, restrictions and behavioural guidelines, what are Islam's teachings regarding ethical practices in commerce and what are their implications? This chapter aims to answer some of these questions by casting light on the Islamic teachings on business conduct, or what has been known since the early Islamic periods fourteen centuries ago as the 'rules of sales and commerce'. It identifies the Islamic business ideals and their practical implications which organizations dealing with Muslim consumers need to adopt.

The Islamic perspective on commerce is increasingly gaining momentum and importance in today's global economy for many reasons. First, Islam, being a practical religion with clear daily procedures to follow, shapes the attitudes and behaviours of its adherents, the Muslim consumers, who represent more than a fifth of the world population. Second, the financial crises of 2008/9 shattered the world markets which had followed conventional financial wisdom, while allowing those practising Islamic finance to prosper and make significant gains. In the September 2008 quarter, when share markets in London and New York were a third of their peaks, Dow Jones's Islamic financials index, in contrast, rose 4.75 per cent. Third, as a result of the oil boom, as well as other factors, many Muslim countries are becoming the most affluent consumers in the world. Fourth, the level of foreign investment in Muslim countries is increasing. Fifth, there is a movement towards forming a Muslim trading bloc, although such a bloc might take some time to materialize. Finally, sixth, there is a strong push towards the Islamization of countries where Muslims are a majority through laying down clear Islamic codes of conduct in all walks of life, and commerce is no exception to this (Saeed et al. 2001).

Moreover, the globalization of the world economy makes it a requirement for world businesses to be familiar with the Islamic perspective on commerce in order to understand the factors shaping the behaviours of Muslim consumers. Businesses that neglect the acquisition and utilization of such knowledge risk alienating a large proportion of their Muslim target market (Saeed et al. 2001). The Islamic religion has a finely tuned set of rules concerning all aspects of life. By recognizing these rules, the knowledgeable firm can not only serve the spiritual needs of the Muslim community but also capture a truly unique position in the Islamic marketplace (Sacharow 1995).

The Islamic Law, Shariah

Islam possesses a religious law called Shariah which governs the life of Muslims and which Muslims consider to be the embodiment of the will of God. This law, which caters to the needs of Islamic society, is essentially preventative and is not based on harsh punishment except as a last measure. The faith of the Muslim causes him or her to have respect for the rights of all others; it aims at preventing transgression against the universe as a whole (the living, the land, the sea and the heavens).

Islam consists of five pillars: affirmation of the faith (*Shahadah*), that is, witnessing that there is no divinity but Allah and that Mohammad is the messenger of Allah; the five daily prayers which Muslims perform facing Makkah (Mecca); fasting from dawn to sunset during the lunar month of Ramadan; making the pilgrimage to Makkah once in a lifetime; and paying an obligatory charity of 2.5 per cent tax on one's capital. Muslims are also commanded to encourage others to perform good acts and to abstain from evil.

> *The term Islam itself is an Arabic word meaning 'submission to God – Allah,' with its roots in the Arabic word 'Salam' which literally means peace. That may come as a surprise to many non-Muslims, whose perceptions of the belief have been distorted by terrorists, many from the Middle East, whose acts in the name of Islam have been condemned by Muslim leaders everywhere.*
>
> *Belt 2002*

Submission to God's will (accepting the Muslim faith) implies that all actions undertaken by Muslims are acts of worship. Thus eating, drinking, socializing, buying, selling, promoting, manufacturing, education and so on have to comply with God's rules. These rules are stated in the Shariah law. According to Islam, God's rules are stated explicitly or implicitly in the Muslims' holy book, the Quran, or in the teachings of Islam's prophet, Mohammad, and it is the responsibility of Muslim scholars to identify these rules and live according to them. These rules apply to commerce as much as they apply to personal purification and cleanliness.

Islam provides either general or detailed instructions about what is permissible and what is not. Detailed instructions are provided on the acts of pure worship such as prayer, pilgrimage, fasting and charity, as well as a multitude of other aspects of life. However, general guidelines are provided in what is referred to by Prophet Mohammad as 'the affairs of your worldly life'. For example, some rules, like forbidding the use of interest rates as a method of making money, represent a general guideline. The responsibility of Muslim scholars throughout the ages is to identify which trade practices fall under this category and to advise Muslims against them or, in addition, provide alternative Shariah-compliant practices.

Companies seeking to engage in business with Muslim consumers need to know these underlying beliefs that drive the Muslim consumers' behaviour. Multinational corporations should be multicultural as well and not simply impose their own culture; they need to adapt their operations to make their Muslim customers, employees, and suppliers comfortable with their practices (Pomeranz 2004). These companies can constructively use the power of religion through accommodating and harnessing Muslim values more effectively when conducting their businesses in the Muslim marketplace (Rice 1999).

In general, all Muslim practices and acts are classified under the following categories.

1.   *Halal*, or permissible. It has three levels:

       o   *Wajib*, or duty; obligatory acts. Failure to perform them is a sin. Duty can be described as the *Core Halal*, without which a firm can't be seen as Shariah-compliant. Implications: firms must perform *Wajib*. Examples include being honest and transparent.

       o   *Mandoob*, or likeable; preferable but not obligatory. Not performing Mandoob is not a sin. Likeable can be described as the *Supplementary Halal*. Implications: do if possible. Examples include being helpful and going the extra mile.

       o   *Makrooh*, or despised; not preferable, discouraged by religion and usually seen as a last resort. Engaging in *Makrooh* doesn't result in a sin unless it leads to one. The most obvious example of *Makrooh* in Islam is divorce! Although it is Shariah-compliant, it represents the border between compliance and non-compliance. It is loathed by society. Implications: avoid if possible.

2.   *Mushtabeh*, or doubted; acts that a Muslim should refrain from because they might be *Haram* themselves or they might lead to *Haram*. Businesses should refrain as much as they can from engaging in doubted activities for the fear of being perceived to be unscrupulous by Muslim consumers. Firms engaging in these activities risk a Fatwa being issued against them.

3.   *Haram*, or not permissible; all acts condemned explicitly or implicitly by the Islamic religion. Engaging in them or in activities leading to them is a sin.

These categories have obvious implications on what companies planning to engage the Muslim marketplace should and shouldn't do. It is of no relevance whether these companies are Muslim or not, what is of relevance is what they should do, i.e., value maximization, and how they do it – by fair play and just dealing. To illustrate, the duty *Wajib* of a company in Islam is to maximize the good of the society as a whole, not profit maximization. Therefore, a company (its personnel) will be committing a sin if it doesn't actively seek societal value maximization. A company however is at ease in choosing the means to do that, as long as those means are not *Haram* (as long as they are permissible or not a sin).

Although profit maximization is not the ultimate goal of trade in Islam, Islam accepts profits and trade and does not aim to remove all differences in income and wealth that may result in various social and economic classes (Beekun 1996). In fact Islam acknowledges that people will differ and that this difference is for a purpose 'It is We Who portion out between them their livelihood in this world, and We raised some of them above others in ranks, so that some may employ others in their work. But the Mercy of your Lord is better than the (wealth of this world) which they amass.' (Quran 43:32).

The implications of these categories on the marketing aspect of business are very thorough and encompass the entire marketing mix for both services and goods. The first component of the conventional marketing mix, e.g., is the product. In Islamic marketing, however, it is the *Halal* product, and the difference between the two is huge. From an Islamic marketing perspective the product that a company sells must be entirely *Halal*. This means that all inputs, processes and outputs must be Shariah-compliant, i.e., the product and all that has been involved in its creation, delivery, and consumption must be environmentally friendly and totally harmless, as Islam clearly prohibits causing harm to anything that God created (all-embracing harmony in the universe). An un-*Halal* or *Haram* product will be very difficult to sell to the Muslim consumer because the Muslim consumer's behaviour is mostly dictated by the common understanding of what is permissible and what is prohibited under the Shariah law. Being Shariah-compliant is the quickest way to promote the company and its products.

Products and acts that might be seen or interpreted as *Makrooh* (despised) or *Mushtabeh* (doubted) will be immensely difficult to sell to Muslims. The same is true for companies producing these products or engaging in such acts. The Muslim consumer is ultra sensitive and the Muslim masses are easily swayed against anything that can be classified as un-Islamic – be it a country, a company, a product, a process and so on. It doesn't matter that most of a certain company's business is legitimate according to the Islamic law, what this law and its adherents take into consideration are all the small business streams that a company is engaged in as part of the business entirety. Just as a drop of oil ruins the taste of an entire tank of pure water, it is enough for one insignificant stream to be not Shariah-compliant for the image of the remaining fully legitimate business streams to be ruined. The bright side of this is that a company will need to purify all of its actions, resources and operations in order to be able to brand itself as Islamic and position itself favourably in the mind of the Muslim consumer. Such purification of the entire company can't be anything but good since it results in value maximization for the community as a whole, including the company itself. For example, a company that produces pork products will find it difficult to sell anything else it produces to Muslims because pork and all that is associated with it is forbidden in Islam. Muslim consumers will not look at how good its other products are but will see only that it manufactures pork products. This image reflection is applicable worldwide, and more so in the Muslim societies, because the numerous religious self-appointed private and public dogwatches operating in these societies relentlessly scan for non-compliance. Any company found to be engaged in anything other than *Halal* will be stamped as un-Islamic, a very costly stigma indeed! It took Coca-Cola 14 years to be removed from the Arab boycott list; engaging in business with Coca-Cola was shunned religiously almost entirely over the Arab and Muslim world. Between the years 1977 and 1991 and prior to the signing of the various Arab-Israeli peace agreements Coca-Cola was banned from trading in the Arab world because the company refused to abide by the Arab League economic boycott of Israel. For decades, this cost Coca-Cola the opportunity to sell its products in Arab countries. By contrast, prior to 1992, Pepsi had abided by the boycott and enjoyed the bounties of the lucrative Coke-less Arab markets in the boycott days. The image of the company was severely hurt that it took Coca-Cola many years after the peace agreements of 1991 to build its brand in the Arab market.

Finally, although achieving the status of Shariah-compliant might seem hard at first sight, it is essential for success in the Muslim market. A compliant company will get a distinctive competitive advantage over the less compliant competitors. Failure to observe these rules means that the company and its brands will be stamped as Shariah non-compliant and thus un-Islamic; an image that no company can afford to have in the biggest unified market in the history of mankind.

Islamic Ethical System

The Muslim ethical system has four sources: the Quran, the sayings and behaviour of Prophet Mohammad, the example set by his companions, and the interpretations of Muslim scholars of these sources. These provide an entire socioeconomic system that guides the behaviour of Muslims. The system stresses the importance of human well-being and good life, religious brotherhood and sisterhood, socioeconomic justice, and a balanced satisfaction of both the material and the spiritual (Chapra 1992).

In economics, Islam supplies a practical programme that includes detailed coverage of specific economic variables such as interest, taxation, circulation of wealth, fair trading and consumption. Islamic law, which is obtained from the sources listed above, covers business relationships between buyers and sellers, employers and employees and lenders and borrowers (Rice 1999).

The Quran provides a balanced view of human motivation; desire for wealth and propensity for greed and selfishness in humans are recognized. However, since business has to be conducted within a social context, Islam introduces rules to control these desires, as well as guide the behaviour of all parties involved. Accordingly, business success is judged not in material terms, but rather by the degree to which the Muslim is able to comply with God's rules.

Muslims prove their worth to God by behaving ethically in the midst of the tests of this worldly life. These tests could take two forms:

1.   *Temptations*, such as making profit through ungodly ways like lending money with interest, or promoting a product that doesn't fulfil as much as possible of the condition of total purity – all that is involved in the production, delivery and consumption of that product must not cause harm to God's creation. By not surrendering to the temptation of making gains at the expanse of the larger community the company will be fulfilling one of the most important guidelines in Islam: 'There should be neither harming nor reciprocating harm' (Prophet Mohammed), 'all harm, whether affecting an individual or a group of people, must be removed' (Rashid Rida cited in Leaman 1995, p. 255). In reference to intoxicating drinks and gambling, God says: 'There is great harm in both although they have some benefit for people, but their harm is far greater than their benefit' (Quran 2:219). These two temptations, although beneficial in part, fail the test of total purity and as such become forbidden.

2.   *Hardships*, such as lack of Shariah-compliant funds to support one's business. A business owner in this case must abstain from resorting to the use of conventional interest-based finance and resort, instead, to more hard work or to more innovative ways such as the possibility of pooling resources within the community or with other shareholders to run and support the business.

Principles Governing Islamic Ethics

In general, Islamic ethics are governed by the following principles, each of which has significant business implications:

1.   *Unity*. God is the sole creator of the universe, and his people should cooperate in carrying out His will (Rice 1999). The implication for businesses is: *one God, then one constitution, the divine constitution*. This constitution is detailed in the Quran, the teachings of Prophet Mohammad and the example set by his companions. The constitution, e.g., prohibits all forms of discrimination among employees, suppliers, buyers or any other stakeholder on the basis

of race, colour, sex or religion. More specifically, since we all are part of the same human-hood and spiritually equal before God, even if not materially equal on earth (Bassiouni 1993), honesty, trust and a relationship between employers and employees that reflects this human-hood need to be developed and encouraged (Wilson 2006). In other words, people are equal partners and each person is a brother or sister to the other (Rice 1999).

2.   *Iman* (faith). In Islam, faith, or *iman*, is the basic motivating factor for believers, and it is this that determines conscience. Hence, business decisions are guided by *iman*, which in practice means following Shariah law, and engaging in what is *Halal*, or permitted, and avoiding that which is *Haram*, or forbidden (Alawneh 1998). The business decision-maker has free choice, but religious principles provide a framework for the appropriate exercise of that choice (Ali and Gibbs 1998).

3.   *Khilafah* (trusteeship). People are God's trustees on the earth. Although this does not mean denial of private property, it does have important implications. For instance, resources, which are God-given and for the benefit of all, must be acquired lawfully and redistributed in the best interest of everyone (A-Faruqi 1976). No one is authorized to harm (destroy or waste) these resources. When Abu Bakr, the first ruler of the Islamic state after Prophet Mohammad, sent an army on an expedition, he ordered the leader of that army not to kill indiscriminately or to destroy vegetation or animal life, even in war and on enemy territory. These God-given resources (everything in creation is God-given) are not seen as a free good, to be plundered at the free will of any nation, any generation or any individual (Rice 1999). The rich and the powerful are not the real owners of wealth; they are only trustees. They must spend it in accordance with the terms of the trust, one of the most important of which is fulfilling the needs of the poor.

4.   *Balance.* Islam teaches Muslims to be moderate in all of their affairs. Chapra (1992) notes that Islam recognizes the contribution of individual self-interest through profit and private property to individual initiative, drive, efficiency and enterprise. However, profit is not the chief motive (Siddiqi 1981). Since Islam places a greater emphasis on duties than on rights, social good or the

benefit of the society as a whole, not profit, should guide Muslim entrepreneurs in their decisions. The argument underlying this stand is that if duties are fulfilled by everyone, then the individual self-interest is automatically controlled and the rights of all are protected (Chapra 1992).

5.   *Justice* or *Adl*. Justice is a central theme in Islam and is required from all parties in all cases. 'O ye who believe! Stand out firmly for justice, as witnesses to Allah, even as against yourselves, or your parents, or your kin, and whether it be (against) rich or poor: for Allah can best protect both. Follow not the lusts (of your hearts), lest ye swerve, and if ye distort (justice) or decline to do justice, verily Allah is well-acquainted with all that ye do' (Quran 4:135). Exploiting employees, abusing power or using a monopoly to overcharge consumers are all condemned (Wilson 2006). However, businesses cannot be forced to sell at a loss or without a profit under the accusation that they are monopolies. On the other hand, employees are responsible for their own actions and cannot simply blame management indiscriminately or claim that which is not rightfully theirs: 'man can have nothing but what he strives for ...' (Quran 53:39). In addition to its clear objective of eradicating injustice, inequity, exploitation and oppression from society, Islam instructs people not to lie or cheat, to uphold promises and to fulfil contracts. Usurious dealings are prohibited, all wealth should be productive and people may not stop the circulation of wealth after they have acquired it, nor reduce the momentum of circulation (Chapra 1992). The commitment of Islam to justice and brotherhood demands that the Muslim society takes care of the basic needs of the poor. Individuals are religiously obliged and encouraged to earn a living and only when this is impossible does the state intervene; Islam greatly values work and clearly discourages dependence on state or on others.

6.   *Free will* (people have the free will to guide their own lives as God's trustees on earth). This free will though is directly linked to accountability; the more freedom a person has the more accountable a person becomes. According to Islam, although people can fully exercise this free will in making decisions, including business decisions, it is a religious imperative to exercise responsibility to those they deal with and, ultimately, to God by observing His rules

on earth (Naqvi 1994). By implementing God's rules Muslims do not lose their individuality, but they become less selfish and more motivated to serve the wider public.

Islamic Values in Business

Islam is an entire way of life, and its guidance extends into all areas of life. It has given detailed principles to guide and control the various economic aspects in the society. Muslims are to recognize that wealth, earnings and material goods are the property of God, and humans are merely His trustees. These principles, which aim at establishing a just society wherein everyone will behave responsibly and honestly, include the following.

Prohibition of bribery or rashwa. According to the teachings of Islam, bribery is a form of corruption and is strongly condemned. The burden is on both those demanding and accepting the bribe and those offering it. All, givers, takers, and facilitators are strongly warned against engaging in this practice. 'Allah's curse be on those who give and those who take bribes' (Prophet Mohammad).

Prohibition of fraud and cheating. Islam stresses the importance of honesty and warns sellers against exaggerating or lying about their products or services. It is forbidden to gain property or wealth by fraud, deceit, theft or other falsehoods. Sellers involved in fraud are committing a sin. Chapter 83 in the Quran (The Dealers in Fraud) contains the following verses:

1.   'Woe to those who deal in fraud.'

2.   'Those who, when they have to receive by measure from men, exact full measure.'

3.   'But when they have to give by measure or weight to men, give less than due.'

Other clear Islamic teachings in this regard include:

1.   'God permits selling but forbids usurious gain' (Quran 2:275).

2.   'O my people! Give full measure and full weight in justice, and wrong not people in respect of their goods' (Quran 11:85).

3.   'Oh ye who believe! Eat not up each other's property by unfair and dishonest means' (Quran 4:29).

4.   'On the day of judgment, the honest Muslim merchant will stand side by side with the martyrs' (Prophet Mohammad).

5.   'Sell the good and bad separately. He who deceives is not of us' (Prophet Mohammad).

6.   'Swearing produces ready sale but blots out blessing' (Prophet Mohammad).

Yusuf Ali (1991, p. 1616, fn. 6011, 6012), cited in Quddus et al. (2009, p. 328), states that:

> Fraud must be taken in a widely general sense ... it is the spirit of injustice that is condemned – giving too little and asking too much. This may be shown in commercial dealings, where a man exacts a higher standard in his own favor than he is willing to concede as against him ... legal and social sanctions against fraud depend for their efficacy on whether there is a chance of being found out. Moral and religious sanctions are of a different kind ... Whether other people know anything about your wrong or not, you are guilty before God.

Prohibition of discrimination. Islam considers all forms of discrimination unjust and opposes it in all aspects of life. 'No Arab has superiority over any non-Arab and no non-Arab has any superiority over an Arab; no black person has superiority over a white person and no white person has superiority over a black person. The criterion for honour in the sight of God is righteousness and honest living' (Prophet Mohammad).

Greater social responsibility. The importance given to community welfare in Islam breathes new life into the concept of corporate social responsibility, and relates it much more closely to the business than what is usual in world business today. An organization's social responsibility in Islam emphasizes its responsibility in three domains: towards its stakeholders, the natural environment and the community. Where stakeholders are involved, e.g., Islam stresses the importance of putting contractual obligations with employees, partners, suppliers or clients in writing in order to protect the rights of all those involved and affected by the dealing, 'And fulfil (every) covenant. Verily, the covenant will be questioned about' (Quran 17:34), 'Give a labourer his wages before his sweat dries' (Prophet Mohammad). The longest verse in the Quran is dedicated to specifically explaining the importance of documentation as a means of reducing conflict and insuring compliance.

Similarly, specific guidelines exist to direct the organization in fulfilling its obligations and responsibilities towards the natural environment. A business engaging the Muslim market is not just a profit-making machine; it is an institution of the Muslim community and thus must abide by its rules or guidelines. These guidelines relate to, among others, the treatment of animals, such as prohibiting animal-based pharmaceutical research and prohibiting causing all kinds of environmental pollution (Beekun 1996). The Quran states: 'Mischief has appeared on land and sea because of (the meed) that the hands of men have earned. That (Allah) may give them a taste of some of their deeds: in order that they may turn back (from Evil)' (Quran 30:41).

In fact, the punishment in Islam for causing ruination could amount to death: 'he who kills a soul without that soul being convicted of killing another, or without being convicted of causing ruination in the earth' (Quran 5:32).

Prohibition of interest. Islam prohibits all interest-based transactions, whether giving or receiving, and whether dealing with Muslims or non-Muslims. Prophet Mohammad says that Allah curses those who pay interest, those who receive it, those who write a contract based on it and those who witness such a contract, 'Allah will deprive usury of all blessing, but will give increase for deeds of charity' (Quran 2:277).

Prohibition of certain earnings. Islam prohibits making earnings from gambling, lotteries and the production, sale and distribution of alcohol.

Prohibition of hoarding. Both money hoarding and goods hoarding are impermissible, 'and there are those who bury gold and silver and spend it not in the Way of Allah: announce unto them a most grievous penalty' (Quran 43:33). People should take only what they need, no more. Moreover, Islam encourages reasonable spending. The word 'spend' is repeated in the Quran 53 times, 'Those who spend (freely), whether in prosperity, or in adversity; who restrain anger, and pardon (all) men; for Allah loves those who do good' (Quran 4:38).

Prohibition of extravagance and waste. A Muslim should be responsible in spending money. Extravagance and waste are strongly discouraged. '[The Servants of Allah are] Those who, when they spend, are not extravagant and not stingy, but hold a just balance between those extremes' (Quran 25:67). 'O Children of Adam! Wear your beautiful apparel at every time and place of prayer. Eat and drink, but waste not by excess, for Allah loves not the wasters' (Quran 7:31).

Payment of Zakat (alms). Every Muslim who owns wealth, more than a certain amount to meet his or her needs, must pay a fixed rate (2.5 per cent) of *Zakat* to those in need. Alms are a method of narrowing the gap between the rich and the poor, and of making sure that the needs of the needy in the society are met.

Payment of charity. Muslims are encouraged to give constantly in charity. Prophet Mohammad said that 'Nobody's assets are reduced by charity.

Cleanliness. Prophet Mohammad says 'Cleanliness invites towards faith (*Iman*) and faith leads its possessor to paradise.' Cleanliness does not just apply to those areas of a business a customer sees; it includes backstage operations, equipment and storage areas as well.

The Biggest Unified Market in History

In the modern world, Muslims – those who embrace Islam and its laws – account for approximately 21.01 per cent or 1,409,139,261 of the entire world population. Muslims also represent a majority in more than 50 countries. This means that more than one person in five heeds Islam's call, embracing the religion at a rate that makes it the fastest growing of all religions on earth. For these people Islam is an intimate personal connection to the same God worshipped by the Jews and the Christians, a source of strength and hope in our troubled world (Belt 2002).

The values that this one fifth of the world's population share are very strong. Islam is equated with identity and defines behaviour in a way that makes 'how' things are done as important as the 'things' themselves, so the gap between belief and behaviour is almost non-existent. A strong sense of community and welfare underpins all activity in the Islamic world, and informs its business ethics (Beekun 1996).

The impressive number of the Muslim population translates into real economic figures, with some Muslim countries today being, by far, among the richest in the world. Moreover, those 1.4 billion Muslims live in economically feasible numbers in almost all countries in the world, with very few countries reporting small Muslim minorities that are hard to capitalize on commercially.

The overwhelming majority of Muslims live in countries that are predominantly Muslim, or in close Muslim communities in non-Muslim countries as minorities, where Islamic laws dominate. Individual and organizational members of these societies have to practise their life in accordance with the rules of the Muslim society in which they live. These rules are necessarily Islamic or being increasingly Islamized as more and more people resort to religion as an identity and as a way of salvation. As the influence of Shariah-compliant supporters increases, the whole society is being driven towards Shariah-compliant laws and regulations. For example, more and more TV advertisements in the Arab world are being produced using animations and cartoons or women wearing head scarves. The traditional reliance on the look of beautiful Arab women wearing non-Islamic outfits to sell, although still having many advocates, is being gradually replaced by more Islamic substitutes under the powerful influence of the more conservative trends in these societies.

The largest Islamic body, the Organization of the Islamic Conference (OIC), is composed of the economies of 57 member states, 50 of which are overtly Muslim. The remaining members have large Muslim populations, although Muslims are not a majority in them. The percentage of Muslims in Russia, e.g., stands at approximately 15 per cent, yet Russia is a member state. India, on the other hand, has a Muslim population of 150 million but its membership into the OIC is blocked by some countries, mainly Pakistan, due to geopolitical reasons.

Those 57 countries have a combined GDP of nearly USD 8 trillion (before the oil boom of 2008). The richest country on the basis of GDP per capita is United Arab Emirates. On the basis of per capita GDP, Qatar is the richest country with incomes exceeding USD 62,299. The recent boom in oil prices has significantly increased these figures in all oil-producing Muslim countries. In 2008, Abu Dhabi, a member emirate in the United Arab Emirates, had a per capita income of USD 75,000, double that of most European countries, and almost double the US figure.

These countries currently import USD 1 trillion worth of products and export USD 1.4 trillion, creating a growing combined market of USD 2.4 trillion.

Although a significant percentage of exports are oil related, both exports and imports span all types of industrial and consumer goods and services.

Implications for Business

Business people should try to conduct their business dealings with practising Muslims whenever possible. This is so for the following reasons:

1.   Practising people seek 'blessing' before 'profit'.

2.   You are less likely to be cheated. Prophet Mohammad says: 'He who cheats is not of us [the Muslims].'

3.   You are more likely to get a better deal. Prophet Mohammad says: 'May Allah have mercy on those who are easy when they sell, easy when they buy … God loves kindness when you deal with any matter.'

4.   In case of dispute you are likely to get off with less harm. Prophet Mohammad says: 'May Allah have mercy on those who are easy when they judge, easy when they sue.'

5.   You are more likely to be treated better. Muslim scholars accept the rule that 'Religion is treatment' which means that how people deals with all others, how they conduct their affairs, how they performs their duties and so on are what makes people religious.

6.   If you receive a present from Muslims or if they invite you to a meal or a social activity, nothing will be expected in return. Bribery is totally forbidden in Islam and therefore practising Muslims will neither give it nor take it.

Practising Muslims are those who strive to comply with the teachings of Islam, such as perform the Muslim daily five prayers, fast the month of Ramadan, give a yearly charity of 2.5 per cent from their wealth and perform pilgrimage to Mecca once in their life time.

How to identify practising Muslims? Look for the following:

1. Long well-maintained beards.

2. If you are dealing with Arabs from the Arabian Peninsula, the long white dress men wear will not touch the ground since men are forbidden from wearing very long dresses, it is considered a sign of pride. Pride is for Allah alone. Prophet Mohammad says: 'Shall not enter paradise anyone who has an atom of pride in his heart.'

3. Oil-based essences instead of alcohol-based perfumes.

4. The words *Allah* (God), *Ma Sha Alla* (what Allah had willed) and *In Sha Alla* (if Allah wills) are repeated very often during greetings and conversations. Even if you don't understand the language of the people you are dealing with, train your ear to recognize these words because they are good indicators of religious commitment. It doesn't matter that these words are in Arabic, Muslims all over the world use Arabic as their language of religion.

5. Practising older Asian and South Asian Muslims in general dye their long beards red or ginger.

6. Don't confuse the short beard of an older man that has been dyed black with a long beard indicating religious commitment; the former indicates longing for a long-gone youth!

7. During meetings, practising Muslims will take breaks to perform their prescribed five daily prayers. They are very strict about performing these prayers at the exact prescribed time (dawn, noon, afternoon, sunset, early night) and they are unforgiving about the timing. A prayer break will be taken no matter how important the issue being discussed or the stage of the discussions.

Conclusion

Islam encourages work in general, and trade and commerce in particular. The Quran states: 'God has made business lawful for you' (Quran 2:275), and Prophet Mohammad says: 'Nine tenths of sustenance is in commerce'. Prophet Mohammad was himself engaged in commerce before prophet-hood. He was a successful businessman known for integrity and he bore the title, 'the trustworthy' (Kattih n.d.).

Islamic business practices and perspectives represent an alternative to the way business is conducted today. Islam requires that traders, both organizations and individuals, achieve a balance between commercialism and humanitarianism, and between profit and social responsibility. Not only does this approach to business conduct provide a solution to the problems of profiteering, customer exploitation, irresponsible corporate governance and environment destruction, it seeks to promote positive aspects of business such as honest conduct, reasonable profit, fair competition, high standard of service culture, business partnership, cooperation, minimum wage for employees and basic consumerism principles such as the right of buyers to return purchased goods (Yusoff 2002).

Glossary

Allah

Allah is the standard Arabic word for 'God'. While the term is best known in the West for its use by Muslims as a reference to God, it is used by Arabic-speakers of all Abrahamic faiths, including Christians and Jews.

Bribery

According to Black's *Law Dictionary*, bribery constitutes a crime and is defined as the offering, giving, receiving or soliciting of any item of value to influence the actions of an official or other person in discharge of a public or legal duty. The bribe is the gift bestowed to influence the recipient's conduct. It may be money, goods, property, preferment, privilege, an emolument, an object of value, advantage or merely a promise or undertaking to induce or influence an action, vote or person in an official or public capacity.

Commercialism

The term is mainly used today as a critical term and refers to the tendency within capitalism to try to turn everything in life into objects and services that are sold for the purpose of generating profit; commercialization, where the value of everything, including such intangible things as happiness, health and beauty become measured in purely commercial, and materialistic terms.

Consumerism

The equation of personal happiness with consumption and the purchase of material possessions. In economics, consumerism refers to economic policies placing emphasis on consumption. In an abstract sense, it is the belief that the free choice of consumers should dictate the economic structure of a society.

Halal

An Arabic term designating any object or an action which is permissible to use or engage in, according to Islamic law. The term is used to describe anything permissible under Islamic law, in contrast to *Haram*, that which is forbidden. This includes human behaviour, speech, communication, clothing, conduct, manners and dietary laws.

Haram

Opposite of *Halal*. Forbidden, or impermissible.

Hoarding

The excess accumulation of commodities, goods or currency in anticipation of scarcity and/or higher prices. Hoarding can be a business strategy similar to monopolization, where an individual or organization attempts to temporarily control available supplies of a given good in order to artificially increase the price. This strategy is also known as 'cornering the market'.

Hoarding of money

The accumulation of money (in the form of gold at the origin) by people who avoid spending it or investing it in economic projects.

Islam

Islam is a monotheistic, Abrahamic religion originating with the teachings of the Islamic prophet Mohammad in seventh-century Arabia. The word *Islam* means 'submission', or the total surrender of oneself to God (Allah).

Islamic business ethics

Rules governing business practices, based on the Islamic principles of jurisprudence.

Mohammad

The central human figure of the religion of Islam, who is regarded by Muslims as a messenger and prophet of God, the last and the greatest law-bearer in a series of prophets starting with Adam. Muslims consider him the restorer of the uncorrupted original monotheistic faith (*Islam*) of Adam, Abraham, Moses, Noah, Jesus, and other prophets. He was also active as a diplomat, merchant, philosopher, legislator, reformer, military general and, for Muslims and followers of several other religions, an agent of divine action.

Muslim

An adherent of Islam is known as a Muslim, one who submits to God. The word *Muslim* is the participle of the same verb of which Islam is the infinitive.

OIC

The Organization of the Islamic Conference, the largest Islamic body. The OIC is an international organization with a permanent delegation to the United Nations. It groups 57 member states, from the Middle East, Africa, Central Asia, the Caucasus, the Balkans, Southeast Asia, South Asia and

South America. The official languages of the organization are Arabic, English and French.

Profiteering

Is a negative term for the act of making a profit by methods considered unethical. Business owners may be accused of profiteering when they raise prices during an emergency for example. The term is also applied to businesses that play on political corruption to obtain government contracts. Some types of profiteering are illegal, such as price-fixing syndicates and other anti-competitive behaviour.

Quran

Also sometimes transliterated as Qur'an, Koran, Alcoran or Al-Qur'an, it is the central religious text of Islam. Muslims believe the Quran to be the book of divine guidance and direction for mankind, and consider the original Arabic text to be the final revelation of God. Muslims regard the Quran as the culmination of a series of divine messages that started with those revealed to Adam, regarded in Islam as the first prophet, and continued with the Scrolls of Abraham, the Torah, the Psalms and the Gospel. The Quran itself expresses that it is the book of guidance. Therefore it rarely offers detailed accounts of historical events; the text instead typically placing emphasis on the moral significance of an event rather than its narrative sequence.

Shariah

This is the body of Islamic religious law. It is the legal framework within which the public and private aspects of life are regulated for those living in a legal system based on Islamic principles of jurisprudence. Shariah deals with many aspects of day-to-day life, including politics, economics, banking, business, contracts, family, sexuality, hygiene and social issues.

Social responsibility

An ethical theory that an entity, whether it is a government, corporation, organization or individual, has a responsibility to society. In business, it means that businesses should function morally and contribute to the welfare of their communities.

Zakat

Almsgiving as an act of worship, the third of the five Pillars of Islam, *Zakat* is an obligatory payment of 2.5 percent of wealth made once a year under Islamic law and is used for charitable and religious purposes.

References

Alawneh, S. F. (1998). 'Human motivation: An Islamic perspective.' *American Journal of Islamic Social Sciences* 15(4): 19–39.

Al-Faruqi, I. R. A. (1976). 'Foreword.' In *Contemporary Aspects of Economic Thinking in Islam*, Indianapolis, IN: American Trust Publications.

Ali, A. J. and Gibbs, M. (1998). 'Foundations of business ethics in contemporary religious thought: The ten commandment perspective.' *International Journal of Social Economics* 25: 1552–64.

Bassiouni, M. C. (1993). 'Business ethics in Islam.' In *The Ethics of Business in a Global Economy*, ed. P. M. Minus. Dordrecht: Kluwer Academic Publishers. 117–22.

Beekun, R. I. (1996). *Islam and Business Ethics*. Herndon, VA: International Institute of Islamic Thought.

Belt, D. (2002). 'The world of Islam.' *National Geographic*. Retrieved 23 February 2011 from http://ngm.nationalgeographic.com/ngm/data/2002/01/01/html/ft_20020101.5.html.

Chapra, M. U. (1992). *Islam and the Economic Challenge*. Herndon, VA: International Institute of Islamic Thought.

Kattih, A. (n.d.). 'Islam and business.' The Islamic Education and Services Institute. Retrieved 27 January 2010 from http://www.2discoverislam.com/projects/business_ethics.htm.

Leaman, O. (2005). *The Qur'an: an Encyclopedia*. London: Routledge.

Naqvi, S. N. H. (1994). *Islam Economics and Society*. London: Kegan Paul International.

Pomeranz, F. (2004). 'Ethics: Towards globalisation.' *Managerial Auditing Journal* 19(1): 8–14.

Quddus, M., H. Bailey and L. White (2009). 'Business ethics: perspectives from Judaic, Christian, and Islamic scriptures.' *Journal of Management, Spirituality & Religion*, 6 (4) 1942-258X: 323–34.

Rice, G. (1999). 'Islamic ethics and the implications for business.' *Journal of Business Ethics* 18: 345–58.

Sacharow, S. (1995) 'Islamic marketing opportunities opening up for converters.' *Paper, Film and Foil Converter*, 1 December. Retrieved 23 February 2011 from http://pffc-online.com/mag/paper_islamic_marketing_opportunities/.

Saeed, Mohammad, Zafar U. Ahmed and Syeda-Masooda Mukhtar (2001). 'International marketing ethics from an Islamic perspective: a value-maximization approach.' *Journal of Business Ethics* 32 (2): 127–42.

Siddiqi, M. N. (1981). 'Muslim economic thinking: a survey of contemporary literature.' In *Studies in Islamic Economics*, ed. K. Ahmad. Leicester: The Islamic Foundation.

Wilson, R. (2006). 'Islam and business.' *Thunderbird International Business Review* 48(1): 109–23.

Yusoff, N. M. A. B. N. (2002). *Islam and Business*. Selangor, Malaysia: Pelanduk.

2

The Islamic Market (*Souq*)

Last month French Finance Minister Christine Lagarde announced France's intention to make Paris 'the capital of Islamic finance' and announced several Islamic banks would open branches in the French capital in 2009. Lagarde said at least three banks had requested permission to operate in France – the Qatar Islamic Bank, the Kuwait Finance House and the Al Baraka Islamic Bank of Bahrain.

AdnKronosinternational 2008

The ethical principles on which Islamic finance is based may bring banks closer to their clients and to the true spirit which should mark every financial service. Western banks could use tools such as the Islamic bonds, known as Sukuk, as collateral. Sukuk may be used to fund the car industry or the next Olympic Games in London.

Loretta Napoleoni and Claudia Segre in L'Osservatore Romano,
3 March 2009

Learning Objectives

After reading this chapter, you should be able to understand:

- Pre-Islamic Arab markets
- The organization of the market (*Souq*) in Islam
- Market manners in Islam
- Islamic markets (primary, secondary, emerging)
- The Islamic product (by compliance, by country, by manufacturer)
- The Islamic company (by product, by location, by ownership, by customer)
- Islamic marketing (by compliance, by scope).

Introduction

The epigraphs at the beginning of this chapter, which are made by some of the most influential thought leaders in the world's economic and cultural arenas, are examples of the growing recognition of the feasibility of the Islamic principles of trade as an alternative, or at least as a complement, to the conventional theories of growth and economic development.

Although the world's attention has until now focused primarily on the specific sector of Islamic finance, this narrow focus is no longer viable due to the unique bases on which Islamic finance is built. Successful implementation of Islamic finance requires that all related activities are Islamic. A bank, or any other company for that matter, cannot create an Islamic brand or position itself as Islamic if it promotes its business through un-Islamic means. The use of the word 'Islamic' to describe a company's operations has huge implications, starting from how the product is developed and ending with how it is handled after final use. Islamic is not just a name, it is an entire business philosophy that incorporates every single aspect of the business.

While this chapter is not dedicated in any way to Islamic finance, it aims to introduce and conceptualize a closely related term: Islamic marketing. Islamic businesses, including Islamic banks and financial institutions, have relied historically on conventional marketing. This reliance played a major role in preventing them from occupying a more advanced place on the world's financial stage. Moreover, Islamic businesses have concentrated on one aspect of the conventional marketing mix: the product. These businesses kept on developing and introducing new products under the Islamic banner and somehow forgot, or came to the false conclusion that having an Islamic product is enough to do business. The other marketing mix components of price, promotion and place have been largely ignored.

The Islamization of the marketing function through applying the principles of Islamic marketing, which are intrinsically ethical, will allow businesses to be more at peace with the world as well as with themselves, in addition to establishing relationships that are honoured by customers with an almost religious zeal.

Islamic marketing addresses the current marketing thought and practice within the overall frame work of the religion of Islam. It studies how the Muslim market's behaviour is shaped by various religious and cultural concepts affecting almost all economic decisions in these markets. Doing business successfully in Islamic markets requires that the prevalent conventional marketing knowledge be tailored to comply with the requirements of Islamic markets. In other words, the current marketing thought and practice needs to wear a turban, a veil or at least a head scarf in order to appeal to these markets. To be more specific, Islamic marketing blends the religious, the ethical and the business worlds to:

1. Create a more humane world market where buyers get a fair deal and sellers accept a reasonable profit, in a better-maintained environment.

2. Help both Muslim and non-Muslim marketers understand the needs of the massive Muslim markets.

3. Provide marketers with current information on the behaviours of Islamic markets and their needs as well as analyze their future trends.

Consumers are fed up with how they have been treated. They want to be seen as humans, not as wallets for marketers to drain. They want products that will keep the planet habitable for their children and their grandchildren. They want marketers who care more about the health and well-being of their consumers. They want companies that view the interest of the community as a minaret that guides their operations, not as a target to shoot at. The ethical principles of Islamic marketing can help greatly in this regard. Businesses that Islamize their entire marketing function will have a tremendous competitive advantage over others that delay such a transition.

The Market (*Souq*)

In Arabic the word *Souq* (sometimes spelt *Souk*; the plural is *Aswaq* or *Aswak*) means the place where selling and sales take place. The name is actually an exact linguistic description of how goods are brought into the market; sellers would *Souq* (herd, shepherd, lead or bring) their goods in. However, the word *Souq* as a concept has been defined during the life of Prophet Mohammad as 'any place where a sale occurs'; it is tied to the transaction itself not to the place. Thus, in Islam, a market is held wherever and whenever an exchange takes place between buyers and sellers under mutually agreed-on terms and conditions.

Pre-Islamic Arab Markets

Pre-Islamic Arabs had many well-known markets, many of which were seasonal and held during specified days. These markets were classified either as local markets serving the neighbouring villages and tribes, such as Souq Hajar on the western coast of the Arabian Gulf, or general markets that people came to from all parts of the Arabian Peninsula, such as Souq Aukaz near Mecca. Some of these markets had greater importance than others due to their geographical location, such as Souq Eden, because they were more involved in international trade with the markets of India, Abyssinia, Persia and China. Other markets such as the Yamamah market gained its importance from being located on a caravan crossroads.

These markets were controlled by princes who imposed tax, tribal chiefs who charged tribute money or local representatives of foreign powers. In general, the goods sold in these markets included dates, raisins, oil, ghee, leather, scents, dresses, weapons and animals. Not all of these goods were sold in all markets since many of them were specialized markets, depending on their location, season, customers, and suppliers.

The greatest motivation for people to attend these markets was that many were held during the four holy months of the Arabic Lunar year, which have been deemed sacred since the days of the Prophet Abraham. Since fighting was forbidden during these months it was safe to travel in the Peninsula, which gave traders and tribes a chance to bring their goods in, trade and return without being harmed.

However, in addition to the trade and safety factors, these markets were a forum for competition in poetry and speech as well as showing pride in ancestry and lineage. Judges attended these markets to judge competitions and to rule on disputes between the tribes or the individuals. Another benefit of these markets, aside from their obvious trade benefits, is that they helped unify the Arabic language, traditions and religion. For instance, for poets in Souq Aukaz to be heard and understood by all Arabs they had to use vocabulary that was acceptable and considered fluent Arabic by all tribes. Since control of trade in the Peninsula during the last few centuries preceding Islam moved from the Yemenis to the Prophet's tribe of Quraish, the tribes came to accept the version spoken by Quraish as the most advanced form of the Arabic language. The military and trade powers of the Prophet's tribe helped make their particular dialect dominant in the entire Arabian Peninsula long before the birth of the

Prophet. That version is the one used in the holy Quran, the teachings of the Prophet, and it is the formal language of all Arabs now.

Although there is no agreement between Arab historians on the exact number, date or duration, Said Al Afghani (1993) counted 20 markets and classified them into three categories:

1. Markets subject to foreign authority. Hajar and Oman were under Persian control while Gaza on the Mediterranean and Busra in Syria were under Roman control. However, all of these markets were run by Arabs appointed by either the Romans or the Persians.

2. Markets controlled solely by Arabs and run by their leaders and nobles. These markets reflected Arab culture and were mostly located deep inland, far away from the threat of the great powers of that era. The best examples are Souq Aukaz near Mecca and Yamamah near Riyadh. Aukaz was abandoned in 746 AD.

3. Mixed markets where the Arabian influence was not particularly strong. These markets were located on ports and merchants from as far as China used to sail in to trade.

The trade activities brought about by these markets greatly affected the Arab lifestyles giving them access to luxuries they were not accustomed to. Arab nobles indulged in fancy clothes, scents, weapons and wine, the last of which they sought to bring from its best-known sources at the time in Syria and Iraq. Pre-Islamic Arabic poetry is full of poems commending wine, wine gatherings and wine servers. It is hard to find a poem that doesn't mention wine in some way or another.

The Importance of Market in Islam

Islam gives a special attention to the market. It urges people to go into markets to trade and make gains. The Shariah clearly urges believers to take trade as a profession and to make money through trading. 'O ye who believe! Squander not your wealth among yourselves in vanity, except it be a trade by mutual consent' (Quran 4:29). Islam also considers trade a way of acquiring of the blessings of God, in one verse in the Quran it was mentioned straight after prayer. 'And when the Prayer is finished, then may ye disperse through the land, and seek of the Bounty of Allah' (Quran 62:10). In another verse, traders were even compared to those who fight in the cause of God: 'He knows that there must be among you sick, and others who travel in the land seeking of the bounty of Allah, and others who fight in Allah's way' (Quran 73:20). And Prophet Mohammad says: 'The one who brings merchandise to our market is like the one who fights in Allah's cause.'

In Islam, believers are not only dwellers in Mosques or monks in monasteries. They are people of profession and trade, although their worldly activities don't take toll on their religious duties. 'Men whom neither merchandise nor sale beguileth from remembrance of Allah and constancy in prayer and paying to the poor their due' (Quran 24:37). The centrality of the market in Islam is expressed in the fact that God counts the market as one of His major blessings on the people of Macca. 'Have We not established for them a sure sanctuary, whereunto the produce of all things is brought (in trade), a provision from Our presence? But most of them know not' (Quran 29:57).

Mohammad, who was a merchant before he became a Prophet, when asked about the best ways to gain, said: 'A sale that is accepted by God and a man working with his hands.' The Prophet used to go to the market to make a living until the non-believers of his time, trying to criticize him, counted that as non-prophet-like behaviour. 'What sort of a messenger is this, who eats food, and walks through the streets? Why has not an angel been sent down to him to give admonition with him?' (Quran 25:7). This criticism, however, didn't deter the Prophet and the Muslim leaders from going into markets sometimes to trade and others to monitor their operations. For example, Abu Bakr, who was the first Muslim caliph, used to trade in garments until the Islamic state gave him a salary and asked him to dedicate all his time to running the newly established state. Omar, the second caliph, said that making deals in the market was the reason underlying his lack of knowledge about a particular matter he was asked to explain. He was also given a salary and told that he was now a caliph not a merchant. One of the most righteous companions of the Prophet later became the richest man in the Islamic state with a staggering fortune of 50 million dirhams. He immigrated from Macca where the followers of the new religion of Islam where prosecuted to Medina where the Islamic state was declared, headed straight into the market to start trading and began making his fortune.

The Organization of Markets in Islam

Markets in Islam were under the Hisbah authority chaired by the market governor or the Muhtasib. The Muhtasib would have a dedicated place – later it became an office – in the market and would have employees assisting him. His duties included continuous inspection and supervision of transactions in the market including terms, conditions, and quality. He would have to be of good character, knowledgeable of both trade and Shariah, and fair. He would ensure that the market operations didn't violate the teachings of Islam.

The Hisbah or market authority was broadly defined by Ibn Khaldun (1332–1406 AD) as a religious job involving asking people to do good and to refrain from doing evil (Khaldun 1967). A more specific definition was provided by Aldraiweesh (1989) as managerial control carried out by the government through dedicated employees who monitor the activities of individuals in the areas of ethics, religion and economy, with the objective of making sure that fairness and virtue as defined by Islam and by prevalent customs at each and every environment and era are achieved.

The Hisbah evolved gradually throughout the Islamic history. The Prophet was the first to monitor and control markets. For example, he saw a pile of foodstuff in the market and he checked it and found that it was wet. He asked the seller why is that and the seller replied that it was rained on. The Prophet asked him to place it on top so that people could see it, and then He said, 'Who cheats on us is not one of us'. In another example, 'In the time of the Apostle of Allah (peace be upon him) we used to be called brokers, but the Prophet (peace be upon him) came upon us one day, and called us by a better name than that, saying: O company of merchants, unprofitable speech and swearing takes place in business dealings, so mix it with sadaqah (alms)' (Hadith,).

The Muhtasib would supervise markets, monitor weights and measures, disperse crowds, and remove obstacles. There are countless examples demonstrating his direct involvement in the market:

1. Standards. A Muhtasib found that a man had mixed milk with water so he ordered it spilled.

2. Pricing. A Muhtasib ordered a man to either increase the price of the raisins he was selling or leave the market.

3.   Pricing. A Muhtasib makes sure that meat must always have a tag price that people could see and that traders couldn't go above.

4.   Location. A Muhtasib removed the oven of a blacksmith because it occupied an area in the market that belonged to everyone and no one had claim to it. The market of the Muslims is like their mosque; he who chooses a place first gets to keep it that day until he leaves.

5.   Exploitation. A Muhtasib used to have a mule that worked for one dirham a day. On a particular day his servant came back with a dirham and a half. When asked how he got the extra half a dirham the servant said that there was much demand and thus he was able to raise the price. The Muhtasib said not true, but you overworked the mule so give it three days off.

6.   Mystery shoppers. A Muhtasib would send unsuspected young boys and girls to the market to buy and then he would weigh the goods purchased to make sure that they were of the correct weight. If a trader was found to mess with the weights and measurements he would be punished severely. If he did it again then he would be expelled from the town.

The Muhtasib system was perfected during the Muslim reign in Spain, which ended in 1495. The system is still used in Spain under the same name.

THE CHARACTERISTICS OF THE MUHTASIB

1.   Public employee. It is a public position filled by an employee appointed by the Muslim leader. A suitable salary is attached to that position.

2.   Duration. It is a fulltime job. A Muhtasib should not take other jobs.

3.   Disputes and complaints. It is his duty to receive and resolve disputes and complaints.

4.   Inspection. It is his duty to look for violations and to remove them.

5. Authority to employ. A Muhtasib can employ assistants to ensure compliance with Shariah in the marketplace.

6. Authority to discipline. A Muhtasib has the authority to discipline those who violate the Islamic rules of the market. However, violators must not be disciplined until the matter is clarified to them.

7. Faith. A Muhtasib must be a Muslim because his main duty it to ensure market compliance with the teachings of Islam.

8. Accountability. A Muhtasib is accountable to the one who appointed him to that position.

9. Gender. A Muhtasib can be a woman in a women's market. The second Muslim caliph appointed Ashshifa, daughter of Abdullah, as a Muhtasib in one of the markets of the Prophet Mohammad's city (Medina).

10. Secrecy. A Muhtasib is better to perform his job in secret if possible. However, if a trader continued after that to violate the rules then he will be ordered publically to refrain from his wrongdoing.

11. Personal character. A Muhtasib must be kind, smiling and well-mannered in order to facilitate communication with traders. The Prophet says, 'Allah, the Blessed and Exalted is kind and loves kindness. He is pleased with it and helps you with it as long as it is not misplaced' (Hadith).

GENERAL DUTIES OF THE MUHTASIB

1. Market accessibility. To monitor roads and paths in the market and ensure that they remain uncongested and their roofs high enough to allow easy access to shops. Shopkeepers are not allowed to exhibit their goods on these paths because such an act is seen as a transgression on pedestrians.

2. Division of market. To divide markets according to the type of the product or service being provided. Those whose professions require the use of fire, such as blacksmiths, cooks and bakers, must have shops located far away from garments and scents shops. The

Muhtasib appoints to each of these divisions supervisors who know the ways of traders in them and their possible violations. The local supervisor would also report to the Muhtasib on prices and on availability of goods in their respective divisions.

3.   Monitoring scales, weights and measures. These must be inspected without the knowledge of sellers in many cases and must weigh or measure at least as much as they should. It is OK to give buyers more but not less, 'Give just measure, and cause no loss (to others by fraud). And weigh with scales true and upright. And withhold not things justly due to men, nor do evil in the land, working mischief' (Quran 26:181–3). A companion of the Prophet also reports the following story, 'I and Makhrafah al-Abdi imported some garments from Hajar, and brought them to Mecca. The Apostle of Allah (peace be upon him) came to us walking, and after he had bargained with us for some trousers, we sold them to him. There was a man who was weighing for payment. The Apostle of Allah (peace be upon him) said to him: Weigh out and give overweight' (Hadith).

4.   Money market. To inspect the money market and to make sure that coins are produced to exact measures and specifications and to ensure that a balance is achieved between the amount of money available in the market and the economic situation in the country to ensure stability of prices.

5.   Deals and transaction. To thwart unlawful deals and transactions and to prevent the sale of products declared impermissible in Islam. Examples of unlawful transactions include, as instructed by the Prophet (peace be upon him): 'The price paid for a dog, the price given to a soothsayer, and the hire paid to a prostitute are not lawful' (Hadith).

6.   Prevention of monopoly. To prevent monopolies and to force traders to sell at equal value if there is a need to do so.

7.   Brokers and middlemen. To oversee the operations of brokers and middlemen and to prevent them from selling until they know who the seller is and to document that information in their books in

order to ensure that what is being sold is not stolen, disputed, taken by force or acquired through any other illegal means.

8.   The production of meat. To supervise the slaughter of animals, making sure that these are free from disease, to prevent butchers from blowing between the skin and the body of the animal when it is being skinned to avoid human breath from changing the flavour of the meet, to ensure the place where the meat is prepared and sold is clean, and that adequate procedures are used to preserve meat.

9.   Women's markets. To appoint trustworthy men or women to supervise women's markets and to prevent men from going into women's markets or sitting in their paths.

Market Manners in Islam

Islam provides clear guidelines for how people, both buyers and sellers, should behave once they are in a market. These guidelines were reflected and expressed in the behaviour of Prophet Mohammad when he entered, organized and supervised trade in the early Islamic markets in Medina where the Islamic state was established. The following is a description of some of these guidelines.

1.   Upon entering a market a person should begin by reciting a prayer praising Allah, acknowledging His unity, and testifying that all good is in His hand.

2.   Once inside a person should not shout or raise his voice. The Prophet Mohammad was described in the Quran as 'You are neither discourteous, harsh, Nor a noise-maker in the markets'(Hadith). Markets should be kept clean. Hygiene is one of the best-known teachings of Islam.

3.   Dwellers in the market are strongly encouraged to greet each other even if they are strangers. The Islamic greeting is 'Peace be upon you'. Greetings are seen as a means for entering paradise. 'You shall never enter paradise until you believe and you shall not believe until you love one another, shall I tell you about something which,

if you do, [will] make you love one another: make salutations common amongst you' (Hadith).

4.   When an armed a person enters the market he should secure his weapon in order not to hurt others. The Prophet asks that 'Whoever passes through our mosques or markets with arrows should hold them by their heads lest he should injure a Muslim' (Hadith).

5.   People should refrain from sitting on roadsides. Women should also abstain from actions that could attract the attention of men such as wearing jewellery and using make up. 'If you have to sit at all, then fulfil the rights of the road … Keeping the eye downward (so that you may not stare at the women), refraining from doing harm, exchanging greetings, and commanding the good and forbidding the evil' (Hadith).

6.   Even if a Muslim is busy running his trade he shouldn't isolate himself from what goes on in his community. He should be an active participant in the community affairs.

7.   A trader needs to be knowledgeable of the art and conduct of trade and of the permissible and forbidden in religion (*Halal* and *Haram*). This is in order to protect him from falling victim to trade misconduct. Omar Ibn Alkhattab, the second Muslim caliph, says 'No one sells in our market accept he who has knowledge of the religion' (Hadith).

8.   The freedom of the market must be protected from all types of transgression. There are many teachings in that regard. After the Prophet chose the location for the marketplace he said 'this is your market, its size shouldn't be made smaller and no tax should be imposed on it.' When one of his companions erected a tent in the new market to sell dates the Prophet ordered that the tent be burned because that act was seen as a transgression on the market as public property where all people are equal and no one has claim. The second caliph did the same with a blacksmith who occupied an extra part of the same market. Moreover, it is forbidden to meet products before they arrive at the market because it is in the market that the price is set between all buyers and all sellers. The prophet clearly requested traders to abstain from hurrying to meet incoming

trade caravans saying 'Do not meet the merchant in the way and enter into business transaction with him, and whoever meets him and buys from him (and in case it is done, see) that when the owner of (merchandise) comes into the market (and finds that he has been paid less price) he has the option (to declare the transaction null and void)' (Hadith). This prohibition is implemented to allow the market to do its job in setting the right price.

9.   False bidding is when one or more would bid higher without an intention to buy in order to deceive the buyer into paying a higher price for the product. This type of behaviour is known in Islam as *Najash* and the Prophet has declared it impermissible.

10. The trade in goods from disputed sources is forbidden. For example, stolen goods and goods taken by force are not accepted into the Islamic market.

Islamic Marketing Defined

The term 'Islamic marketing' can be understood in several ways. It can be seen as religion-based marketing, marketing within Islamic markets or marketing to or from Islamic markets. Each of these views has its defining characteristics and implications. However, in order to appreciate the difference between them the terms 'Islamic market', 'non-Islamic market', 'Islamic products' and 'Islamic company' need to be understood.

THE ISLAMIC MARKET

In general, an Islamic market is where the target consumer is a Muslim. A Muslim consumer is one who is a follower of the religion of Islam. Although this definition is broad enough to include Muslim countries as well as Muslim communities in non-Muslim countries, it fails to account for the emerging segment of non-Muslim consumers adopting Islamic products. A more precise definition of the term 'Islamic market' would be one that accounts for Muslim majorities, minorities and non-Muslim consumers of Islamic products. More precisely, the Islamic market is composed of primary, secondary and emerging.

Primary Islamic markets

This is a market where the majority of the population of a country or a region follows the religion of Islam. Currently, these countries are members of the Organization of Islamic Conference (OIC). The OIC has a membership of 57 states representing Asia, Africa and Europe. In these markets the word *Halal* is not commonly used since it is taken for granted that all available products are *Halal*. These markets can be classified as the primary Islamic markets where the majority of consumers are Muslims and the products sold are *Halal*.

Secondary Islamic markets

The Islamic market is also composed of significant Muslim minorities in most countries of the world. These minorities range from a few hundred million in India to a few thousand in some of the newly independent states. Contrary to the situation in Islamic states, the catchword for these minorities is *Halal* and all shops and service providers add this word on their business signs. For example, in addition to the sign that says OPEN, another one next to it will say HALAL. The word *Halal* in these markets is sometimes overused as a marketing tool. To illustrate, a colleague of mine saw a sign beside a street seller in the UK that read *Halal Miswak*. A *Miswak* is a branch of a certain tree used by Muslims as a natural toothbrush! In this case, as in many others, there is no need to advertise the product as being *Halal* since there is no *Haram Miswak*; a *Miswak* is *Halal* by nature. This example, however, describes the state of affairs in these minorities where a less than adequate understanding of Islam prevails and, at the same time, shows the strength of the religious appeal of products in minorities where the concept of identity might be associated with consuming or being affiliated with certain products or consumption patterns.

Emerging Islamic markets

A small yet rapidly evolving market for Islamic products is comprised of some of the adherents of other religions in non-Muslim countries. This growing segment represents consumers who have been exposed to *Halal* products in their home country. For example, many of the customers of the British Islamic Bank, which is a fully Shariah-compliant bank, are Christians. Many of the customers of *Halal* shops in Western countries are not Muslims. Some go to these shops because they claim the flavour of meat sold there is different due to the strict Islamic guidelines detailing how an animal should be prepared for consumption, some go there for the experience of being in a shop that is different, stuffed with all of these exotic products and strange brands, and run by different people, while others go there because of the influence of living in or near Islamic communities.

NON-ISLAMIC MARKETS

Non-Islamic markets are those where the target consumers adhere to religions other than Islam. This definition includes, in addition to countries where the majority of the population is not Muslim, non-Muslim minorities in Islamic countries. For example, 3 per cent of the population in Jordan is Christian, about the same percentage of the population in Egypt is Coptic Christian and nearly 40 per cent of the population of Malaysia is non-Muslim. There are non-Muslim minorities in almost all Islamic countries. None-Islamic minorities' markets are sometimes similar to Islamic markets in their consumption patterns. Christian minorities in the Arab world are a good example. In fact, judging by the consumption patterns of these minorities, it is very difficult to know who is a Christian and who is not. All of them consume *Halal* products.

THE ISLAMIC PRODUCT

An Islamic product can be understood in three ways: according to Shariah-compliance, place of production or manufacturer.

Shariah-compliant products

These are products that are manufactured and promoted as Shariah-compliant, i.e., *Halal*. They are produced and consumed mainly in the primary and secondary Islamic markets and they are rarely known in non-Islamic markets. However, many non-Islamic multinationals produce *Halal* brands that are specifically destined to Islamic markets. Many of Nestlé's products are being produced according to *Halal* principles and are being heavily advertised and distributed to Muslim consumers in both secondary and primary Islamic markets. The same products can be found on the shelves of numerous stores in non-Islamic markets since making these products Islamic required minimum changes to the production process, or the use of alternative yet similar ingredients.

Products produced in an Islamic country

These products are produced in an Islamic country. Their classification as such is based on the location where they are being manufactured. Almost all of these products are *Halal* since they are destined for local or regional Islamic markets. Only a small portion of them is exported to secondary Islamic markets. These products are not promoted as Islamic and the descriptions 'Islamic' and '*Halal*' are almost never mentioned. This is due to the fact that the word 'Islamic' is understood from a religious perspective among Muslims and these companies never intended to be understood as religious companies. There is no need for such a concept.

On the other hand, some of the products produced in Islamic countries are actually un-Islamic, including alcoholic beverages, cigarettes and indecent media materials. These, of course, cannot be classified under this category of products.

Products produced by an Islamic company

These products are produced by an Islamic company. Mecca Cola which is supposed to rival Coca-Cola is produced by a company that capitalizes on Muslim sentiments to make gains in the marketplace. The company promotes itself as an entirely Islamic company. However, an examination of the brand name Mecca clearly reveals that the choice of the name Mecca is un-Islamic in the sense that it is demeaning to a very secret Islamic place. The company clearly went too far in commercializing a purely religious concept. This was recognized later when people began seeing piles of empty bottles of the 'Islamic Soft Drink' with the name Mecca highly visible on them scattered around trash containers.

THE ISLAMIC COMPANY

An Islamic company, much like an Islamic product, can be understood in different ways: according to the type of its products, its location, its ownership or its intended customers. It can be a specialized company producing Shariah-compliant products, a company located in an Islamic country, a company owned by Muslims regardless of its location or a company producing mainly for Islamic markets regardless of its ownership.

Islamic company by product

Companies that specialize in the production or distribution of products that comply with the teachings of Islam, i.e., *Halal*, are classified as Islamic companies. These companies might be located anywhere and owned by anyone. The key differentiating criterion in this category of companies is that their products are manufactured as Shariah-compliant. Clearly, their main target market is consumers in one or more of the three types of Islamic market: primary, secondary and emerging.

Islamic company by location

Companies whose main business operations are located in Muslim countries are also considered as Islamic companies, regardless of their type of ownership or customer base, which could be a mixture of both Islamic and non-Islamic customers. Examples of companies that qualify for this category include the Saudi dairy producer MARAI, SABIC and ARAMCO, the Emarati Etisalat and Dubai Ports and the Egyptian Orascom and Ceramica Cleopatra. Although the bulk of these companies' businesses are Shariah-compliant, some caution is necessary since some of the companies classified in this category specialize in producing or providing un-Islamic goods or services. A good example would be the commercial banking sector which provides interest-based financial services, an absolutely forbidden business in Islam. Another example would be all the alcoholic beverages businesses located in the various Islamic companies.

Islamic company by ownership

Companies owned by Muslim shareholders are classified sometimes as Islamic companies. However, one should be careful in making this assumption since many of these companies have operations that are un-Islamic or non-Shariah complaint. Casinos, wineries, nightclubs, bars and betting businesses owned by Muslims shouldn't be classified as Islamic since their core business is totally outlawed by the religion of Islam. To relate these businesses to Islam and to classify them as Islamic would create a paradox since Islam strongly condemns all of their activities, profits and personnel.

Islamic company by customer

Companies that produce to capitalize on and meet the needs of Muslim consumers, regardless of the location of these consumers, or the location of the companies themselves and their types of ownership are also classified as Islamic. Nestlé is being increasingly perceived among Muslim consumers as being an Islamic company because the company Islamized nearly 70 per cent of its production operations, i.e., uses *Halal* processes and ingredients.

This category of companies could also include Islamic-friendly companies. Pepsi-Cola was once perceived by Muslim consumers as being supportive to Muslims because it abided by the Arab boycott of Israel, in contrast to Coca-Cola which decided not to abide. More recent examples of companies stamped as un-Islamic are Danish companies in general because of the drawings which were published by a Danish newspaper, which Muslims interpreted as demeaning to Mohammad, the Prophet of Islam. This stigma has lost Danish businesses that have major business operations in Muslim countries much of their market share and cost them dearly.

Religion-based Marketing: Shariah-compliant Marketing

Within Islamic markets, adding the word 'Islamic' to marketing will be understood to mean Shariah-compliant practices, i.e., adhering to the teachings of Islam regarding all facets of trade, applying Islamic business ethics and observing the market manners as dictated by the religion of Islam. A good demonstration of this understanding is the clear differentiation that exists between commercial banks and Islamic banks in the Muslim world. Prior to the establishment of the first Islamic bank in the late 1960s only one type of bank existed as far as Muslims were concerned. These banks implemented the Western banking system and practices and had no provisions to incorporate the specific needs of the increasing number of practising Muslim consumers who were reluctant to deal with non-Islamic banks. Before that time the market didn't envision a need to provide an alternative financial system that would cater to the needs of the increasingly affluent Muslim consumer. As such, banks were known to be only the banks. However, once the sector of Shariah-complaint banking and finance emerged there was a need to differentiate this newly thriving business stream from conventional banking. The new banks are now known as Islamic banks.

Another example of religion-based marketing is Al-Islami Cooperative brand in the United Arab Emirates where the product is *Halal*, the owners and customers are locals, and the location is within a Muslim country.

The marketing strategies of companies pursuing religion-based marketing are based on the religious appeal and the power of religion to attract. The words *Islam* and *Halal* are clearly visible in the marketing campaigns that are carried out by these companies.

Local Islamic Marketing: Marketing within Islamic Markets

This type of marketing is concerned with the practices that are carried out by marketers within the Islamic markets and directed mainly at Muslim consumers. All marketing activities are aimed at consumers within the primary and secondary Islamic markets. No noticeable efforts have been made yet to direct these activities at the emerging Islamic markets, i.e., non-Muslims buying Islamic products. The typical seller and buyer are Muslims. The brands that are being advertised are mostly *Halal*, the brand owners are most likely to be Muslims and the location is either local or regional, i.e., the Middle East, North Africa or any single Islamic country or Islamic community in a non-Islamic country. This type of marketing is sensitive to culture but not necessarily based on religion. The words *Islam* and *Halal* are rarely used in the marketing campaigns of companies in this category. It is highly likely that these firms will remain local; very few of them will be significant players in international markets that are different in terms of culture and religion.

International Islamic Marketing: Marketing To or From Islamic Markets

Marketing activities in this category are carried out by multinational companies targeting Muslim consumers in the various Islamic markets, or by Islamic companies targeting international markets outside the Islamic market. When a company (by product, location, ownership or location, as defined earlier) markets outside of the Islamic world it is classified as an Islamic company and its activities are interpreted as such, i.e., Islamic. The criterion used to classify these companies as Islamic is based on their location. Although they are classified as Islamic, they might not be using the Islamic marketing principles as outlined by the religion of Islam.

On the other hand, marketing activities carried out by multinationals targeting Islamic markets are classified as Islamic only because their target consumer is either a primary or secondary Islamic market. Since these companies were not established in the first place to serve the Muslim consumer and since the particular needs of the Muslim consumer were recognized much later by them, many of their operations, processes and products remain Shariah non-compliant. Some of the companies that trade with the Islamic world manufacture both *Halal* products intended for Islamic markets and almost identical, yet non-compliant, products intended for non-Muslim customers.

Multinationals usually ignore the emerging Islamic market for several reasons. These markets are difficult to identify and reach and in many cases they are not sizeable enough to be visible to serve. Moreover, specially designed marketing campaigns need to be developed to target them which might push prices sharply up.

Conclusion

The pre-Islamic definition of a *Souq* or *Souk* used to be an actual designated place where selling occurs. However, the Islamic concept of a market is much more inclusive because it is tied to the transaction itself, not the place. It is defined as anywhere and any time a sale occurs. Pre-Islamic Arabs, endowed with a strategic location, were professional traders and had many well-known markets including Souq Hajar, Souq Aukaz, Souq Marbad and Souq Eden among many others located on various trade routes in Iraq, Syria, Yemen, Bahrain, Oman and what is now known as Saudi Arabia. These markets served as a place where goods from China, Africa and Europe were traded, in addition to being a meeting place where people from various cultures interact. Although these markets played a central role in unifying the Arabic culture and language, many of them where under the authority of the major neighbouring powers of that time, such as the Persian and the Byzantine empires.

Islamic marketing, on the other hand, addresses the current marketing thought and practice within the overall frame work of the religion of Islam. It studies how Muslim markets' behaviour is shaped by various religious and cultural concepts affecting almost all economic decisions in these markets. Doing business successfully with Islamic markets requires that the prevalent conventional marketing knowledge be tailored to comply with the requirements of Islamic markets. In other words, the current marketing thought and practice needs to wear a turban, a veil or at least a head scarf in order to appeal to these markets.

When Islam established its state in the Arabian Peninsula the organization of these markets became a priority to all Muslim leaders, beginning with the Prophet Mohammad himself who was a merchant prior to Prophethood. Many of the Muslim caliphs also were merchants before becoming heads of state. There are numerous verses in the Quran and teachings in the Sunnah that guide adherents on how to organize their markets and conduct their trade. In the Islamic state a market governor, Muhtasib, was appointed to oversee the overall operations of the market and to ensure that all deals and transactions were conducted in line with the teachings of Islam, i.e., no monopoly, no cheating, fair price, standard weights and measures, no exploitation of people, land or animals, and so on. The Muhtasib, although appointed by the state, was a fully independent job and its decisions were not influenced by anyone in the State. It was very much like the position of a judge. Being such a demanding and sensitive job the Muhtasib had to be a man or a woman of good character as well as have deep knowledge about markets and how they operate. Islam provides clear guidelines for how people, both buyers and sellers, should behave once they are in a market. These guidelines include special prayers, greetings, lowering one's voice, hygiene, handling of arms and responsibility towards community, as well as many others.

The concept of Islamic marketing can be understood in several ways. It can be seen as religion-based marketing, local Islamic marketing or international Islamic marketing. Each of these has its defining characteristics and implications. Closely related terms to Islamic marketing include 'Islamic market', 'non-Islamic market', 'Islamic products' and 'Islamic company'. Each one of these terms can also be understood in several ways. An Islamic market in general, e.g., can be divided into primary, secondary and emerging markets while non-Islamic markets can be defined as those where the target consumers adhere to religions other than Islam. An Islamic product could be one that is Shariah-compliant, produced in an Islamic country or produced by an Islamic company. An Islamic company could be one that specializes in producing Shariah-compliant products, is located in an Islamic country, is owned by Muslims regardless of its location or is producing mainly for Islamic markets regardless of its ownership.

Glossary

Souq

An Arabic word that means the place where selling and sales take place. The term is often used to designate the market in any Arabized or Muslim city.

Caliph

The caliph is the head of state in a caliphate, and it is the title of the leader of the Islamic *Ummah* (nation), an Islamic community ruled by the Shariah. It is a transliterated version of the Arabic word *khalīfah* which means 'successor' or 'representative'.

Hisbah

The *Hisbah* (verification) is an Islamic doctrine of keeping everything in order within the laws of Allah. This doctrine is based on the Quranic expression 'enjoin what is good and forbid what is bad'. In a broader sense, *Hisbah* also refers to the practice of supervision of commercial, guild and other worldly affairs.

Muhtasib

A Muhtasib was a supervisor of trade in the Islamic countries. His duty was to ensure that public business was conducted in accordance with the law of Shariah. Traditionally, a Muhtasib was appointed by the caliph to oversee the order in marketplaces, in businesses, in medical occupations, etc. For example, during the reign of the Sultan Barquq of Egypt (died 1399 AD), the duties of the Muhtasib of Cairo included the regulation of weights, money, prices, public morals and the cleanliness of public places, as well as the supervision of schools, instruction, teachers and students, and attention to public baths, general public safety and the circulation of traffic. In addition, craftsmen and builders were usually responsible to the Muhtasib for the standards of their craft (Donald 1984). 'The Muhtasib also inspected public eating houses. He could order pots and pans to be re-tinned or replaced; all vessels and their contents had to be kept covered against flies and insects. The Muhtasib was also expected to keep a close check on all doctors, surgeons, blood-letters and apothecaries.' (Stone 1977). A Muhtasib often relied on manuals called *Hisbah*, which were written specifically for instruction and guidance in his duties; they contained practical advice on management of the marketplace, as well as other matters a Muhtasib needed to know such as manufacturing and construction standards.

Primary Islamic market

A market that is composed of Muslim consumers. Currently this market includes the OEC member states.

Secondary Islamic market

A market that is composed of Muslim minorities in non-Muslim states.

Emerging Islamic market

Non-Muslim consumers adopting Islamic products.

Non-Muslim markets

All non-Muslim consumers in the world. It also includes non-Muslim consumers living as minorities in Muslim countries.

Islamic company by product

Companies producing Shariah-compliant product.

Islamic company by location

Companies located in Islamic countries.

Islamic company by ownership

Companies owned by Muslims.

Islamic company by customer

Companies producing for Muslim consumers.

Islamic product by Shariah-compliance

Shariah-compliant products.

Islamic product by production in an Islamic country

Products produced in an Islamic country.

Islamic product by production by an Islamic company

Products produced by an Islamic company.

Religion-based marketing

Shariah-based marketing.

Local Islamic marketing

Marketing within Islamic markets.

International Islamic marketing

Marketing to or from Islamic markets.

References

AdnKronosinternational (2008) 'France: Senate looks at easing limits on Muslim finance.' 23 December. Retrieved 23 February 2011 from http://www.adnkronos.com/AKI/English/Business/?id=3.0.2846242034.

Aldraiweesh (1989). Market Rules in Islam. Alam Alkutub Publishing, Riyadh, 1st edition.

Hill, Donald. (1984). *A History of Engineering in Classical and Medieval Times*. New York: Routledge.

Ibn Khaldun (1967) *Muqaddima*, ed. and trans. F. Rosenthal. Princeton, NJ: Princeton University Press.

Said Al Afghani (1993). *Arab Markets in Jahiliayah and in Islam*. Kuwait: Alauruba Publishing House.

Stone, Caroline. (1977). 'The Muhtasib', *Saudi Aramco World*, September/ October. pp. 22–25

.

PART 2

The Islamic Marketing Mix

3

The Islamic Product (*Tayyibat*)

he allows them as lawful what is good (and pure) and prohibits them from what is bad (and impure) ...

Quran 7:157

Eat of the Tayyibât (good lawful things) wherewith We have provided you, and commit no transgression or oppression therein ...

Quran 20:81

Allah has prescribed certain obligations for you, so do not neglect them; He has defined certain limits, so do not transgress them; He has prohibited certain things, so do not do them; and He has kept silent concerning other things out of mercy for you and not because of forgetfulness, so do not ask questions concerning them.

The Prophet Mohammad

Learning Objectives

After reading this chapter, you should be able to:

- Differentiate between an Islamic product and a conventional product
- Understand the principles guiding product decisions within an Islamic context
- Understand the *Tayyib*, the *Khabeth*, the *Halal* and the *Haram* and their guiding rules
- Understand the Islamic product hierarchy
- Understand the concept of harmful products and the Islamic legislation for their disposal.

Halal … or Not Halal

Whilst food and drinks must be *Halal,* or Shariah-compliant, most technology and other products don't need to be classified as *Halal* products. Examples include mobile phones, watches, jewellery, transportation, and so on. Nonetheless they are heavily promoted and sold as Islamic products. What makes them 'Islamic' is that they are branded as part of the identity of the Muslim and that they support the Islamic cause and believes. Mecca Cola was not branded as *Halal* but as an Islamic product that came in a time when emotions among Muslim consumers were running high. It was not branded as *Halal* because its competitor Coca-Cola was not branded by Muslim activists as un-*Halal* – or *Haram* – but as un-Islamic.

Halal, as will be explained throughout this chapter, indicates that a product has been prepared according to the Shariah principles using Shariah-compliant ingredients and processes. An Islamic product, on the other hand, is one that inspires Muslims to be more 'Muslim' and one that is associated with a Muslim's ambitions, hopes and search for an identity in a time where when such an identity proves elusive.

Introduction

In the Arabic language, which is the language of the Quran, Sunnah and related Islamic literature, the words used to describe the English terms of products, commodities and goods are (1) *Tayyibat,* (2) *Rizq,* (3) *Mataa,* (4) *Zenah,* (5) *Sel'ah,* and (6) *Bezaa'ah.* These words, which are sometimes used interchangeably in studies pertaining to the Islamic economic system, are contextually and conceptually different to their counterparts in conventional marketing, where the words 'commodities' and 'products' represent abstract descriptions of benefits offered to customers – that is in the marketing mix, a product is defined as a good or service that most closely meets the requirements of a particular market or segment and yields enough profit to justify its continued existence (Businessdictionary 2010). The Islamic alternative terms, aside from *Sel'ah* and *Bezaa'ah,* which are similar in their meaning and use to those in the English language (goods), go much deeper than the abstract and the materialistic to describe the richer spiritual and psychological associations of the offering. The term *Tayyibat,* e.g., refers to *purity, wholesomeness* and *lawfulness* while the term *Rizq* (sustenance) refers to the source of the *Tayyibat,* Allah, who also describes himself as *Tayyib* and who is the sole and undisputed provider of sustenance.

The *Rizq* is used to denote the following meanings: Godly sustenance, divine bestowal, godly provision and heavenly gifts.

The terms *Mattaa* and *Zenah* describe the worldly uses or purposes of these products. *Mataa* comes from an Arabic word which means fun and joy while *Zenah* refers to products as means of beautification and adornment.

These key differences that distinguish the Islamic marketing perspective from that of conventional marketing and which manifest themselves in the terms used to describe the 'product' have a profound impact on all product-related decisions beginning with the choice of the brand name, functionality, styling, quality, safety, packaging, repairs and support, and warranty, and ending with the associated accessories and services. To add more, the Islamic perspective on the product, aside from addressing the conventional tangible and intangible aspects is governed by what is called in Shariah, *Maqasid* (aims), which in this particular case deals with the overall consequences of the creation, consumption and disposal of the product in both the short and the long run.

While the terms *Sel'ah* and *Bizaa'ah* are used in Arabic as generic terms without any connotations; the terms *Mataa* and *Zenah* need to be used with care to avoid any association with extravagance, which is condemned by the teachings of Islam. On the other hand, *Tayyibat* and *Rizq* can be used without restrictions, assuming of course that the product is *Halal* in the first place.

The Product in Conventional Marketing

In order to be able to appreciate the unique view Islam provides on all economic matters, including marketing and the marketing mix, one must first understand how conventional marketing has viewed these issues, including the product as part of both the concise (4Ps)[1] and the extended marketing mix (7Ps or 8Ps[2] depending on which writer you are reading). In conventional marketing literature and practice the word 'product' has been mostly defined based on its level of tangibility where offerings having mostly tangible attributes are classified as goods and offerings having mostly intangible attributes are classified as services. This distinction between the two is more of a continuum rather than a dichotomy (Lefkoff-Hagiusl and Mason 1990) and is hardly applicable in the highly developed marketplaces of today since

---

1   Product, price, promotion and place.
2   Product, price, promotion, place, process, productivity, people and physical evidence.

it is very difficult to find a product that can be marketed solely based on its tangible attributes, which represent the actual attributes within the three levels of the product: core (intangible), actual (tangible) and augmented (intangible) as shown in Figure 3.1.

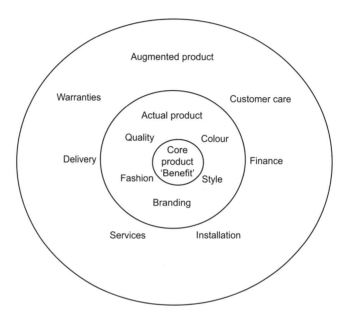

Figure 3.1   The three levels of a product

While tangibility refers to the physical existence and discernibility of attributes or features such as colour, size and weight through one or more senses, intangibility has been defined in terms of the abstract, beneficial and subjective attributes of the product. Using an illustration from (Lefkoff-Hagiusl and Mason 1990, p. 137) 'a car can be described as large, red and luxurious. Large and red are fundamentally tangible attributes as they describe physical properties of the car, while luxurious is primarily an intangible attribute as it describes beneficial and imagery aspects of the car.'

The Tayyibat

To understand the word *Taiyyib* (masculine; *Taiyyibah* is feminine) correctly we need to understand its uses in the Arabic language, which are quiet varied.

A land is *Taiyyibah* if it is good for plantation, a wind is *Taiyyibah* if it is soft and gentle, a meal is *Taiyyibah* if it is *Halal*, a woman is *Taiyyibah* if she is righteous and honourable, a word is *Taiyyibah* if it is good in itself and if it doesn't imply bad, a town is *Taiyyibah* if it is safe and prosperous, a flavour is *Taiyyibah* if it is free from foulness. A human who is *Taiyyib* is one who has shed the badness of ignorance, bad deeds and wrongdoing and has become learned and well mannered with good deeds. A scent is *Taiyyibah* if it free from unpleasant odour. For example, a food is *Taiyyib* if it has been acquired from where it should have been and as it should have been acquired, in the right quantity, in the right place, with the right company and in the right time. To summarize, the term *Taiyyib* (masculine), *Taiyyibah* (feminine), *Taiyyibat* (plural feminine) or *Taiyyibeen* (plural masculine) describe everything that senses enjoy. These terms, even in pre-Islamic markets, were never used in Arabic to describe certain products such as alcohol, prostitution services, donkey meat or slavery businesses, all of which were declared illegal during the life of Prophet Mohammed (570/571–632 AD). The term has such a gentle and kind connotations to it that made pre-Islamic Arabs refrain from using it to describe alcohol and pork, e.g., although it could be easily argued that these appeal to the senses of many people.

Although pre-Islamic Arabs used it correctly, a complete understanding of the full meaning of the term *Taiyyib* cannot be achieved without understanding how it has been shaped by Islam. From the Islamic religious perspective, *Taiyyibat* can be defined as the goods and services that are Shariah-compliant. It is the plural of *Taiyyib*, which is the opposite of *Khabeeth*: 'Say (O Muhammad): Not equal are *Al-Khabîth* (all that is evil and bad as regards things, deeds, beliefs, persons and foods) and *At-Taiyyib* (all that is good as regards things, deeds, beliefs, persons, foods), even though the abundance of *Al-Khabîth* may please you. So fear Allâh, O men of understanding in order that you may be successful' (Quran 5:100).

In Islam, 'products' are associated with values and ethics. The word *Taiyyibat*, which is mentioned in the Quran 18 times, has been explained by Islamic scholars to carry the meanings of beauty, purity, physical and spiritual cleanliness, and attractiveness, and it is usually used along with the word *Rizq* (sustenance). Because in Islam Allah is the sole sustainer (*Razzaq*) and because He is *Taiyyib* then *Rizq* –which is provided by Him – can be nothing else but *Taiyyib*. Therefore, Muslims are obliged by the teachings of their religion to make *Taiyyib* everything that they do, including each and every single action leading to or involved in the making of the product.

Islamic scholars, who cannot be called scholars unless they are also knowledgeable about the Arabic language, have introduced several closely related definitions of what *Taiyyibat* means. *Kahf*, cited in Alrummani (n.d.), defined them as: 'the useful and beneficial material granted by Allah to his servants. The consumption of these leads to material, ethical, and spiritual *benefits* to the consumer.' Turkumani (1990) defined Taiyyibat in a similar manner but emphasized in the last part of the definition that the consumption of these leads to material, ethical, and spiritual *meanings*. These definitions make it clear that *Taiyyibat* is what a Muslim can benefit from in accordance with the Shariah guidance and that *Khaba'ith* (plural of *Khabeeth*) is all that which cannot benefit a Muslim in a Shariah-compliant manner under normal circumstances. Under other circumstances, however, *Khaba'ith* can be made use of or consumed but within the limits of 'absolute necessity'. For example, a Muslim is allowed to consume 'just enough' of a non-Shariah compliant product, i.e., *Haram*, pork, e.g., to allow him to survive if he could not find any other source of food and his survival was clearly at risk. Once this necessity is lifted the licence to consume is cancelled and consumption of that particular product becomes a sin.

The definitions also indicate that all products that do not result in material, ethical or spiritual gains for the Muslim consumer will be classified as *Khaba'ith*. There is no such thing as consumption for the sake of consumption itself in Islam. All consumption decisions must generate a benefit that is accepted as 'benefit' under the teachings of Islam. The absence of these benefits would render a product as *Khabeeth* (singular of *Khaba'ith*).

The distinction in Islam between these two categories of products has significant implications for both producers and consumers. Needless to say, Muslim consumers are not allowed to consume any product that is not from the *Taiyyibat* and violation of this rule without a religiously accepted necessity would result in a sin that might be punishable within the Islamic legal system. For example, the punishment for the consumption of alcohol is a certain and predetermined number of lashes. Smuggling drugs on the other hand is punishable by death while the punishment for drug dealers begins with severe financial or physical punishment and ends with death for repeat offenders (IslamQA 1986; Turkumani 1990).

Since Muslim consumers are not allowed to consume *Khaba'ith* then it would not make any economic sense for producers to produce such products. In addition to the lack of economic visibility, producers are ethically bound to produce *Taiyyibat* and to refrain from the production of *Khaba'ith*, even if what they produce is aimed for non-Muslim markets. The Islamic rule is very clear in this regard and it doesn't distinguish between a Muslim and a non-Muslim market, it is universal in nature.

However, if by some chance *Khaba'ith* enter the Islamic market, i.e., a market that observes the teachings of Shariah, they will be rapidly disposed of and thus the market remains a place where only the pure, good and beautiful products are traded. According to the Islamic teachings, *Khaba'ith* (bad, impure and unclean products) are not considered consumables, which must be *Taiyyibat* (good, pure and beautiful) and therefore (Ibn-Aljawzi n.d.):

1.   They should not exist in the Islamic market.

2.   They cannot be priced; they are valueless and worthless.

3.   They cannot be considered possessions because Muslims are not allowed to own them.

4.   They cannot be considered wealth for Muslims and therefore losing them is not to be compensated.

In the case of non-Muslims consuming *Khaba'ith* within an Islamic market, if these are considered lawful according to their own religion, then their right to consume them is protected by the Shariah law. For example, a Christian in an Islamic state is allowed to consume alcohol and pork but this cannot be done through any transactions with Muslims, simply because it is not lawful for Muslims to trade in these products (Kahf n.d.). In Dubai, e.g., there are three conditions for acquiring a liquor licence, in addition to being an expatriate:

1.   Earning in excess of AED 3,000 per month (about US$ 820).

2.   Being a resident in Dubai.

3.   Being a non-Muslim.

The application process takes two weeks with an application fee of AED 160 and requires the approval of the applicants sponsoring company. The licence allows a holder to consume alcohol for one year after which it must be renewed. In addition, liquor stores and shops cannot be owned, or operated by Muslims. It is completely off-limits for them by both civil and by religious laws. However, it is worth noting that this doesn't stop some Muslims from consuming the product.

Although so far all products were classified as either *Taiyyibat* or *Khaba'ith*, it must be made clear that *Khaba'ith* cannot be considered products from an Islamic perspective. In Islam only that which is Shariah-compliant can be referred to as product. Any 'product' that by its nature is a cause of harm, whatever form or shape that harm might take, is a forbidden 'product'. The word harm in this context is defined as what people consider harmful and what Islam considers harmful and, if there is a disagreement between the two, then the final say is what Islam says. 'And whatsoever the Messenger gives you, take it; and whatsoever he forbids you, abstain (from it) And fear Allâh; verily, Allâh is severe in punishment' (Quran 59:7).

To conclude, *Khaba'ith* is either considered harm or a cause of harm and Islam provides the following guidelines on how to deal with harm:

1.   The removal of harm is a Shariah obligation.

2.   Its removal must not involve the use of harm.

3.   Specific or limited harm is tolerated for the sake of removing public harm.

4.   The least of the two harms is committed in order to avoid the other.

5.   Avoidance of harm is given priority over the acquisition of benefits.

Classification of Products in Islam

The discussion has so far concentrated on clarifying the difference between lawful and unlawful products from an Islamic perspective. However, lawful or *Taiyyibat* productes have been classified by Islamic scholars into four different levels, which are depicted in what is called the hierarchy of products in Islam as shown in Figure 3.2. These levels are *Dharuriyyat* (necessities), *Hajiyyat* (needs), *Kamaliyyat* (improvements) and *Tarafiyyat* (extravagances), which are *Halal* by nature but might be *Haram* by use. Each of these needs has many implications from a purely business perspective. For example, a company's image could be severely tarnished within an Islamic market if that image is closely associated with the production of *Tarafiyyat*.

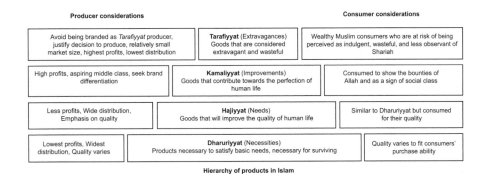

Hierarchy of products in Islam

Figure 3.2   Hierarchy of products in Islam and their implications for procedures and consumers

DHARURIYYAT OR NECESSITIES

The concept of staying alive in Islam extends well beyond the conventional concept of survival and encompasses the preservation of the five basic pillars of life, that is: faith, body and soul, mind, honour and wealth. Those correspond to a minimum amount of food and drink, clothing, basic transportation, medication and health services, literacy, security to one's life, honour, wealth and books. Within an Islamic economic system these products are given priority and in the case where the market fails to produce enough the state steps in to ensure their availability to all citizens within the state. Once the market has reached equilibrium, production planning gives priority to the next type of products on the hierarchy, or the *Hajiyyat*.

HAJIYYAT OR NEEDS

These correspond to basic products as stated previously but differ in quality, amount and availability. While it is the state's duty to ensure that all citizens get enough necessities, it is the religious responsibility of the people themselves to move higher up the hierarchy, which in turn enables them to get better quality and larger amounts at their convenience or whenever they wish, in addition to other appliances that make one's life easier. Examples of products at this level include better food, higher-quality clothes, a larger home, home appliances, bottled water instead of tap water, suitable public transportation, vocational and higher education, books of all titles and counselling services.

KAMALIYYAT OR IMPROVEMENTS

The third level of the Islamic product hierarchy involves the satisfaction of the five pillars of life using products of a higher order. For example, owning a beautiful house in an upscale area, private transportation, expensive schooling for children, and so on. At this level the brand name becomes much more significant in product adoption and use.

Although a faithful Muslim cannot go beyond this level in his efforts to achieve satisfaction, it is his religious duty to show and demonstrate the bounties that Allah has bestowed on him by eating well, dressing beautifully and humbly enjoying the blessings of Allah. In fact, enjoying these gifts from Allah is a good deed that is even rewarded by Allah in both this world and the hereafter. This enjoyment is a form of showing gratitude to the Allah, the one who gave in the first place and a means of generating more blessings. To explain, if Allah grants a certain wealth to a person yet that person decides to hide it or block its use, that persona would be considered ungrateful. Allah gives wealth to be used not to be buried: 'And remember! Your Lord caused to be declared (publicly): If ye are grateful, I will add more (favours) unto you; but if ye show ingratitude, truly My punishment is terrible indeed' (Quran 14:7).

Nonetheless, it is important to know that *Kamaliyyat* is a boundary area; that is, one must not exceed what is considered a form of gratitude by consuming or acquiring that which definitely doesn't make one's life clearly better. There is no need to get a second car if one is enough. There is no need to have several TV sets at home, extravagance aside, these will limit communication between family members and slowly destroy the concept of a family since everyone will want to sit alone and watch his own TV show as he pleases and without interruption from others, even though those others are his family. A few pairs of shoes will do nicely, why get a whole closet full of them? Why buy all the vegetables in the market when one knows that most of it will end up thrown away, in addition to creating unreal demand, which in turn needlessly drives prices up and aggravates the suffering of the less advantaged in society?

Having said that, it should be clear though that Islam makes allowances for individual and cultural differences. It acknowledges that what might be considered pure extravagance in one culture might be seen as an improvement or even a need in another. While a servant is a necessity for a person with disability – during the height of the Islamic state a servant was appointed to guide blind people on their way to mosques – it is an act of extravagance for someone who already has enough servants, cannot afford them or cannot treat them in accordance with teachings of Islam, which are very detailed and give the servant a long list of rights and make him or her almost a family member.

The tipping point from improvements and into extravagancies gets closer with each extra purchase that cannot be justified from a religious perspective. It is exactly this point that producers should disassociate themselves from because the description of consumption beyond it enters the forbidden zone of *Tarafiyyat*, or more religiously put, showing ingratitude to Allah who expects people to use what he provided for them to benefit life as a whole not for self-indulgence.

To conclude, it is clear from the discussion above that producers are safe operating at the first two levels of the Islamic product hierarchy, need to practise caution when operating at the third level, and should be very clear on how their product is classified in the particular Islamic market in which they are operating when it comes to producing products that could be considered *Tarafiyyat*. As a general rule, producers should carefully consider the following guidelines when prioritizing what to produce:

1.   The importance of these products in strengthening faith among Muslims. As discussed in this book, Nestlé and other multinational corporations are actually making Muslims more observant because they are making them more knowledgeable about which international brands are compliant with the teachings of their religion.

2.   Their importance in maintaining social security.

3.   Their importance in the preservation of physical and mental health.

4.   Their role in supporting society, through job creation for example.

What are *Haram* Products?

Although this book is concerned with the guiding Shariah rules to Islamic marketing, providing a list of basic *Haram* products would help readers, both Muslims and non-Muslims, appreciate the fact that only a small fraction of all available things is actually forbidden by Shariah. Before doing that though, readers should be aware of the Islamic principles governing *Halal* and *Haram*:

1.   Permissibility of things is the rule, prohibition is the exception.

2.   To permit and to prohibit is the right of Allah alone.

3.   Prohibiting the *Halal* and permitting the *Haram* is wrongdoing.

4.   The prohibition of things is due to their impurity and harmfulness.

5.   What is *Halal* is sufficient, while what is *Haram* is superfluous.

6.   Whatever is conducive to the *Haram* is itself *Haram*.

7.   Falsely representing the *Haram* as *Halal* is prohibited.

8.   Good intentions do not make the *Haram* acceptable.

9.   Doubtful things are to be avoided.

10.   The *Haram* is prohibited to everyone alike.

11.   Necessity dictates exceptions.

As explained, the list is really short. The following verse from the Quran includes many of them:

> Forbidden to you (for food) are: *Al-Maitah* (dead animals – cattle – beasts not slaughtered), blood, the flesh of swine, and that on which Allâh's Name has not been mentioned while slaughtering (that which has been slaughtered as a sacrifice for others than Allâh, or has been slaughtered for idols) and that which has been killed by strangling, or by a violent blow, or by a headlong fall, or by the goring of horns – and that which has been (partly) eaten

by a wild animal – unless you are able to slaughter it (before its death) – and that which is sacrificed (slaughtered) on *An-Nusub* (stone-altars). (Forbidden) also is to use arrows seeking luck or decision; (all) that is *Fisqun* (disobedience of Allâh and sin). This day, those who disbelieved have given up all hope of your religion; so fear them not, but fear Me. This day, I have perfected your religion for you, completed My Favour upon you, and have chosen for you Islâm as your religion. But as for him who is forced by severe hunger, with no inclination to sin (such can eat these above mentioned meats), then surely, Allâh is Oft-Forgiving, Most Merciful. (Quran 5:3)

In general, what is *Haram* in Islam could be summarized thus:

1.   Animals killed as outlined in the verse above.

2.   Dead animals and their products.

3.   Pig products.

4.   All intoxicating products.

5.   Gold and silverware.

6.   Silk and gold for men.

7.   *Riba*, or charging interest on lending money.

All commercial activities related to these categories of products are to be avoided. For example activities related to the production, distribution, sale and consumption of liquor are forbidden and engaging in any of them is considered a bad deed. Companies need to position themselves as far away as possible from activities associated with these products and their ingredients, producers, distributers both wholesalers and retailers, promoters and consumers.

Finally, these few basic categories of *Haram* products have subcategories that naturally change with time due to factors such as production technologies, inventions, changing consumption patterns and so on. To illustrate, the use of new enzymes and preservatives which were made available by new production technologies, or the introduction of new entertainment means, will also be declared either *Halal* or *Haram*. This declaration is the outcome of a very strict Islamic ruling process leading to the issuance of fatwa stating the permissibility of a particular ingredient, process or a pattern of consumption in light of the teachings of the Sharia principles. Updated lists of these newly developed products could be easily obtained by visiting Islamic websites or contacting *Halal* certification agencies, Islamic studies departments in universities and Islamic endowments ministries in Islamic countries.

Conclusion

An established principle in Islam is that the things which Allah has created – all things are created by Allah – and the benefits derived from them are basically permissible. Nothing is *Haram* except what is prohibited by Shariah through its two main sources, the Qur'an and the Sunnah (practice or saying) of Prophet Mohammad. If these two sources don't explicitly state the prohibition, the original principle of permissibility applies.

In Islam the sphere of prohibited things is very small, while that of permissible things is extremely vast. There is only a small number of texts concerning prohibitions, while whatever is not mentioned in a religious text as being lawful or prohibited falls under the general principle of the permissibility of things and within the domain of Allah's favour. In this regard the Prophet (peace be on him) said: 'What Allah has made lawful in His Book is *halal* and what He has forbidden is *haram,* and that concerning which He is silent is allowed as His favor. So accept from Allah His favor, for Allah is not forgetful of anything' (Hadith).

Trend-setting companies pursuing opportunities in Islamic markets will not only keep abreast of the effects of technology and other factors on the ingredients and processes of production of products destined for the Islamic market, they will lead and create these effects and thus notably differentiate themselves from other companies. Companies that are happy operating within their own comfort zone and avoiding the Islamic market deprive their stakeholders of the massive yet real opportunities that await in the Middle, Near and Far East.

Key Terms:

- Islamic product
- Conventional product
- The *Tayyib* product
- The *Khaba'ith* product
- The *Halal* product
- The *Haram* product
- The Islamic product hierarchy
- *Dharuriyyat* (necessities)
- *Hajiyyat* (needs)
- *Kamaliyyat* (improvements)
- *Tarafiyyat* (extravagances).

References

Alrummani, Z. M. (n.d.). 'The concept of Rizq Taiyyibat in Islam.' Retrieved 30 April, 2010, from http://www.darululoom-deoband.com/arabic/magazine/1173849312/fix3sub4file.htm.

Businessdictionary. (2010). 'Definition of product.' Retrieved 24 April 2010, from http://www.businessdictionary.com/definition/product.html.

Ibn-Aljawzi (n.d.). *The Picnic of the Eyes*. Beirut: Alrisalah Foundation.

IslamQA. (1986). 'Fatwa: Punishment of drug dealers.' Retrieved 30 April 2010, from http://www.islamqa.com/ar/ref/129484.

Kahf, M. (n.d.). 'Islamic economics.' Retrieved 30 April 2010, from http://monzer.kahf.com/books/arabic/al-iqtisad_al-islami_ilman_wa_nizaman.pdf.

Lefkoff-Hagiusl, R. and C. H. Mason (1990). 'The role of tangible and intangible attributes in similarity and preference judgments.' *Advances in Consumer Research* 17: 135–43.

Turkumani, A. K. (1990). *Islamic Economic System*. Jeddah, Saudia Arabia: Sawadi Library.

4

Islamic Pricing Practices

*Allah is the One Who fixes prices, Who withholds, Who gives lavishly,
and Who provides, and I hope that when I meet Him none of you will have
a claim against me for any injustice with regard to blood or property.*

Prophet Mohammad

Acknowledgement

I would like to acknowledge that the works of the Islamic scholars Yusuf
Alqardawi, mainly his book *The Halal and the Haram in Islam*, and Monzer
Kahf's many works on Islamic economics proved to be particularly important
throughout the writing of this chapter.

Learning Objectives

After reading this chapter, you should be able to understand Islam's views on
pricing including:

- The role of the market in setting prices
- Pricing and sellers' right to set prices
- Pricing and consumers' right to acquire necessities
- Pricing as a covenant between the buyer and the seller
- Pricing as a shared responsibility between buyers and sellers.

Consumers as Price Setters

The true spirit of Islamic teachings on pricing can best be illustrated in the following story that happened during the early days of the Islamic state. The companion of the Prophet, Jareer Ibn Abdullah (died circa 671 AD), said 'We made a covenant to the Prophet, may peace be upon him, that we listen and obey and give advice to all Muslims'. Jareer, may Allah be pleased with him, sent his servant to buy a horse. The servant found a horse for 300 dirhams and brought it back along with the seller so that his master could complete the purchase and give the seller the money. When Jareer saw the horse he estimated that it was worth much more than the agreed price; he told the seller that the horse was worth more and offered the seller 400 dirhams. The seller agreed. Then Jareer offered 500 and the seller agreed again. Jareer kept on raising the price until it reached 800 dirhams and gave that amount to the seller. The servant was bewildered by the act of his master and asked him why did he do that? Jareer explained that he made a covenant to the Prophet to give advice to all Muslims and therefore that was the only right thing to be done: to inform the seller, his Muslim brother, the accurate price of the horse.

The longest verse of the Qur'an deals with commercial contracts involving immediate and future payments:

> O you who believe! When you contract a debt for a fixed period, write it down. Let a scribe write it down in justice between you. Let not the scribe refuse to write as Allâh has taught him, so let him write. Let him (the debtor) who incurs the liability dictate, and he must fear Allâh, his Lord, and diminish not anything of what he owes. But if the debtor is of poor understanding, or weak, or is unable to dictate for himself, then let his guardian dictate in justice. And get two witnesses out of your own men. And if there are not two men (available), then a man and two women, such as you agree for witnesses, so that if one of them (two women) errs, the other can remind her. And the witnesses should not refuse when they are called (for evidence). You should not become weary to write it (your contract), whether it be small or big, for its fixed term, that is more just with Allâh; more solid as evidence, and more convenient to prevent doubts among yourselves, save when it is a present trade which you carry out on the spot among yourselves, then there is no sin on you if you do not write it down. But take witnesses whenever you make a commercial contract. Let neither scribe nor witness suffer any harm, but if you do (such harm), it would be wickedness in you. So be

afraid of Allâh; and Allâh teaches you. And Allâh is the All-Knower of each and everything.'

Quran 2:282

Introduction

This chapter does not discuss the pricing strategies applied by global marketers today and it does not determine the permissibility of these strategies from an Islamic perspective. Readers who are looking for a pricing strategy checklist will not find it here and will not find it anywhere else, simply because such a list doesn't and will never exist. All pricing strategies that are commonly used in the marketplace are time-bound! They are variable and change with time and according to market conditions. At any certain point in time some of them will be more important than others while some will be obsolete altogether. Therefore, restricting the discussion in here to these strategies will not be of much help because it will deprive companies from the true benefits that a better understanding of the Muslim consumer could yield. Checklists work well with tools and machines, not with consumers.

Rather than presenting a seemingly attractive, yet oversimplified checklist, this chapter provides timeless guidelines for setting pricing strategies, an approach that is in line with the core teachings of Islam. There is a story narrated about the Prophet Mohammad, peace be upon him, in which he ordered his companions not to pollinate female palm trees and the crop failed the next year; it ends with the statement by the Prophet: 'You are more knowledgeable about your worldly affairs.' Therefore, it would not be Islamic to say that there is a set of predetermined Islamic pricing strategies for marketers to abide by; it is truer to say that there are predetermined guidelines which help Muslim sellers and buyers establish a healthy relationship. These guidelines could be used by marketers to develop pricing strategies that suit their particular market circumstances and, at the same time, comply with the aims of the Shariah which are supposed to ultimately lead to establishing a Godly planet that is governed by equality, peace, tranquillity and prosperity.

Although the discussion above might seem idealistic and vague, and the goals might appear to be too big to ponder about achieving them, the rules provided by the Shariah makes this task a whole lot easier because they draw the road map not to an unachievable market utopia but to market as an organization built around humans and managed by them.

The Market as a Price-setting Mechanism

Since Islam accepts markets as the basic coordinating mechanism of the economic system in the Islamic state its teachings seek to guarantee the flow of goods and services between the consumers and suppliers of this market at a mutually agreed and acceptable price. The Islamic teachings begin with stressing that trade is a welcome activity and that all traders and consumers should be allowed to engage in free exchange within the market. It also protects private ownership against all kinds of transgression whether by the state itself or by competitors or consumers and it incriminates violations of all valid contracts – those that do not violate Islamic teachings. In fact, the longest verse of the Quran deals with commercial contracts involving immediate and future payments.

In principle, the Islamic market should be free to respond to the market forces operating within it and reflecting the aggregate influence of buyers and sellers on the price and the quantity of the offered products. Thus, when Mohammad was asked to set the price of goods in a market he responded, 'I will not set such a precedent, let the people carry on with their activities and benefit mutually …' This Hadith clarifies that unnecessary interference in the freedom of individuals is considered an injustice from which one – whether government, private institution or individual – should distance himself from so that one should meet Allah free the guilt of unwarranted interference in the market.

However, if any artificial forces, such as hoarding and manipulation of prices, interfere in the natural operation of the market, public interest takes precedence over the freedom of the parties behind this interference. In such a situation price control by the Muhtasib – the market supervisor in an Islamic market – becomes permissible in order to protect consumers from unethical pricing practices.

Muslim scholars are mostly in agreement that the prohibition of price control is restricted by the prevailing market circumstances and subject to the general Islamic rules of removing harm and preventing injustice. In other words, price control may at times be unjust and prohibited, and at other times may be just and permissible; it all depends on the nature of these circumstances. If price control results in the sale of goods at an unacceptable price that denies traders the reasonable profit permitted by Allah, interference and price control becomes *Haram*. If, on the other hand, price control leads to equity in the market, e.g., by making sellers accept a price equal to that set by other comparable products, then that control is *Halal*. It is important to know here that a comparable product includes not only the final offering but all activities involved in making that offering or product available to the Muslim consumer including country of origin, logistics, quality and so on. *Sei'ru elmithl* or 'the price of the equivalent' is the term used to denote the price of these products, a price that is referred to when the price of a product is disputed. Accordingly, if a product was being sold without any wrong-doing or unethical market practices but the price rose due to uncontrollable factors such as scarcity then, price control, if practised, would need to be done in a way that doesn't deny traders their reward for bringing this product into the market.

Nonetheless, price control is most likely to take place when the well-being of the society is put at risk and basic products such as education, medicine, food, clothes and shelter are most likely to be subject to such a control. For example, cashew nuts, which are considered mostly a luxury or extravagance product, are more likely to be 100 per cent subject to market forces while bread, sugar, rice and other basic sustenance products will be subject to more monitoring and price controls. This difference between products that are more or less likely to be subject to price controls has significant implications for companies working within the Islamic markets since it affects their margins and mark-ups and their promotion practices.

Sellers' Right to Set Prices vs. Consumers' Right to Acquire Necessities

A company must recognize that, in an Islamic market, market forces are free to dominate only until the 'freedom' of the consumer is put at risk, e.g., jeopardizing the consumer's right to healthy food, suitable medication or proper education. Once these or other rights that are considered by the Shariah as undisputed, natural and acquired by birth are threatened the Islamic state is obliged to end the threat. Therefore, companies should be aware that their ability to manoeuvre within this market is subject to the products they sell and to the type of their operations, e.g., if they operate at the high end of the market at the *Tarafiyyat* or extravagancies level – see Chapter 3 – they will most likely be free to set their prices but if they operate at the basic product levels such as those mentioned above then there is always a possibility of restrictions on operations and limits on setting prices.

Within the Islamic market, the concept of freedom – including the freedom to set prices – can be described as responsible freedom, the concept of unlimited and unrestricted freedom as expressed in the free market philosophy is rejected in all dealings among people. In a market sense, more freedom for one means less freedom for another. If a seller has total freedom then a buyer will not have a choice other than to submit to the seller's will, otherwise how can a seller be described as being totally free if he cannot enforce his freedom? A free market assumes that the power of buyers is equal to that of sellers thus creating market balance, which could not be further from the truth since there are very few examples in the history of business on this planet when buyers were actually able as a mass to take action; they are usually left at the mercy of traders whose objective is mainly to profit, although it is not so plainly expressed.

In conclusion, responsible freedom in Islam as opposed to the freedom granted to traders in a free market, translates into responsible pricing where the sellers' right to make profits does not affect he buyers' rights to a decent life.

The Covenant Between the Buyer and the Seller

Three terms are used in the Quran to describe transactions between people themselves and between people and Allah. These are *Mithaq* (covenant), *Ahid* (also covenant) and *Aqid* (contract; the plural is *Auqood*). In Islam all Shariah-compliant transactions are covenants approved by God and must be honoured by all those who agreed to their terms. These transactions become religious obligation and therefore must be fulfilled regardless of the involved parties. There are many verses in the Quran and numerous teachings by Prophet Mohammad that encourage the fulfilment of covenants and contracts. For example: 'Verily, the covenant will be questioned about' (Quran 17:34), and the opening of Sura Ma'edah or Chapter 5 in the Quran: 'O you who believe! Fulfil (your) obligations' (Quran 5:1).

Although covenants tend to describe the Godly part in the human affair while contracts deal with the much more materialistic part of that affair, together they create a Godly affair, i.e., transaction that is witnessed and approved by God. As such, all parts of that affair must be pleasing to God – Allah – including price or its equivalent in the case of commercial transactions. Putting it more simply, buyers and sellers do not transact with each other, they transact with God. In other words, a seller doesn't transact with a buyer, he transacts with God, and a buyer doesn't transact with a seller, he transacts with

God. Since Allah becomes the first party to the exchange, the second party – the seller or the buyer – is obliged more than ever to purify all aspects of that exchange and endeavour to the best of his ability as a human being to please Allah. The second part to the exchange must exercise and embody qualities that are commonly overlooked among traditional buyers and sellers. These qualities include, but not limited to, generosity, kindness, eagerness to help others gain from the dealing, and easy dealing. Prophet Mohammad gives a clear guideline in this regard: 'May Allah's mercy be on one who is generous (pliable, propitious, good-hearted) when he buys, generous when he sells, and generous when he sues).'

All parties to the exchange are required to make sure that they all benefit, it would be un-Islamic for anyone of them to gain while knowing that another will lose. It is a must in Islam that such knowledge is shared and that all parties are informed about all matters that might affect their decision to engage in the exchange. No information is to be held in this regard: 'He who is asked something he knows and conceals it will have a bridle of fire put on him on the Day of Resurrection' (Prophet Mohammad).

The Buyer–Seller Shared Responsibility for Pricing

A central teaching is Islam is that 'One of you will not be a believer until he likes for his brother what he likes for himself' (Prophet Mohammad). Within the business context this Hadith commands both sellers and buyers to have compassion for each other or, in other words, to put themselves in each other's shoes. Before settling on a price or a price range a seller must think of himself as a buyer and then determine what equitable price he would be willing to pay for the product bearing in mind that he knows its total cost to him as a seller and that he knows its real worth in economic value. Only then he should proceed with setting the price: setting a price that he would like to pay himself.

The responsibility for pricing doesn't end at the seller's end; the buyer is equally responsible. The buyer should put himself in the seller's place and then determine the equitable price he would be setting for the product. Both the buyer and the seller must also be willing to engage in a win–win exchange were the buyer allows the seller to make sufficient gains and the seller allows the buyer to acquire the desired product without being burdened by too high a price or total costs.

Adding the religious dimension to pricing as shown above transforms the buyer–seller relationship and its various dimensions into a religiously rewarding and mutually beneficial one. Sellers' prices will no longer be seen as exploitive and consumers will no longer think of themselves as being the subject of this exploitation. The prevailing enmity and mistrust between the two will be replaced by a relationship of trust and support, the two most important ingredients of business continuity.

Implication for Businesses

Businesses operating in Muslim markets need to pay special attention to how they set their prices and in what price levels to operate. They must:

1.   Demonstrate and create the awareness that their prices are fair to them, to consumers, and to the world. These prices must not lead to the depletion of natural resources or result in ruination in the earth. Such ruination could be pollution, extravagant consumption patterns, moral degradation, and so on.

2.   Avoid excessive profit margins since these could be misinterpreted to be unfair or greedy, two traits that are strongly condemned in Islam.

3.   Since Muslim markets, like all other markets, are composed of consumers with varying purchasing powers, a company could build goodwill by providing good quality products at affordable prices to the less advantaged among those consumers.

4.   Consumers in the Muslim market are weary of the prevalent – but not necessarily Islamic – bargaining nature of these markets. Even consumers who get good deals seem to think that they have not done so. That is one of the reasons why big retailers such as Carrefour are thriving in these markets. Their fixed prices provide comfort and peace of mind to their Muslim consumers who otherwise would have negotiated the price of most of their purchases. Although the sign 'Bargain Shop' might be alluring in the West where such shops are a rarity, it is counter productive in the Muslim market where consumers are under the impression that they are the losing party in this affair.

Conclusion

In line with the teachings of Islam which greatly value the traits of forgiveness and generosity in all affairs, Muslim consumers are compelled to be flexible in their dealings and might even tolerate a higher price if a good cause is presented, such as financial difficulties the seller is facing or the fact that the seller is known to support a religious-related cause. However, marketers are warned that the same teachings ask customers to be vigilant and to avoid being exploited. This presents a pricing challenge for sellers since the line between exploitation by sellers and a fair and equitable price is mostly subjective and in many cases blurred. A company's pricing strategies should be distanced from the fuzzy pricing range where a price might seem to be exploitive of consumers' needs or their unawareness. In a Muslim market where almost all matters are judged from a religious point of view a price that is perceived to be unfair by the masses becomes un-Islamic by definition, which will also stamp dealings with the seller that are not absolutely necessary as un-Islamic.

Although higher margins are allowed, many Muslim scholars suggest that a margin of 30 per cent or less would result in a fair price. In a market where the Muslim consumer understands and lives the Islamic values the market will be free from extravagant purchase and consumption patterns and thus the government need not interfere in setting prices as a way to control market forces. The market can be left to operate independently and freely from such interference.

It is the religious duty of sellers and buyer to act responsibly. The seller is to be generous and giving when determining the price of his offering and the buyer is asked to be no less generous and giving when purchasing such an offering. The relationship between the two is not based on the price level, it is based on whether God is pleased with it or not. The Generous, which is one of God's 99 names in Islam, commands generosity and forbids stinginess. A seller's concern must not be seen to be selling at the highest possible price and the buyer's concern must not be that of dragging down the price. Based on their joint responsibility to set prices, sellers and buyers must strive towards setting a fair price that above all pleases God, the Fair and Just God. Such a price acknowledges the seller's right to profit and the buyer's right to acquisition.

Key Terms:

- Pricing covenant
- Pricing responsibility
- Price-setting
- Sellers' rights
- Consumers' rights
- Fair price
- Excessive profit
- Purchasing power.

5

Islamic Promotions and Promoting to Muslims

Satan makes them promises and creates in them false hopes, but Satan's promises are nothing but deception.

Quran 2:120

For a long time, Muslim consumers have been taken for granted in marketing strategies, and it is time to start designing communication messages that are culture-relevant and more sensitive to their needs …

Roy Haddad, chairman and CEO of JWT MENA

Learning Objectives

After reading this chapter, you should be able to:

- Understand the principles guiding promotions within an Islamic context
- Understand the transformation of the holy marketers
- Understand the importance of promotions as promises
- Understand the implications of extended accountability
- Know what should or should not be included in your marketing campaigns.

Nike Learning about Islam

The example of Nike is a good example of the importance of being sensitive to others' believes. In 1997, a row broke out after Nike used a logo meant to look like flames on a line of basketball shoes to be sold in summer 1997, with the names 'Air Bakin', 'Air Melt', 'Air Grill' and 'Air B-Que'. Some Muslims claimed that the logo resembled the word 'Allah' written in Arabic script. Fearing a boycott by Muslim consumers, the company had to withdraw nearly 40,000 pairs of the shoes worldwide. The immense pressure that Nike was under aimed, according to the Council on American–Islamic Relations' (Cair) executive director 'to reinstate confidence in our community that whenever they see something offensive, there could be something done about it.' Nike's reaction to the campaign against its new line of products was to immediately divert supplies away from Islamic countries and to discontinue production. It had also introduced a review panel into its development process to prevent any similar problems in the future. 'We have, through this process, developed a deeper understanding of Islamic concerns and Islamic issues ... as our brand continues to expand, we have to deepen our awareness of other world communities.'

Nike had to recall all shoes carrying the logo that was perceived to be offensive to Muslims. In exchange for the sales ban, a donation of a USD50,000 playground to an Islamic elementary school in the United States, and an apology, Cair urged Muslims around the world not to boycott Nike products (Jury 1997).

Not long before that, Nike had been criticized by the council for a similar issue. In 1995, the company had to remove a billboard near the University of Southern California that depicted a basketball player with the headline 'They called him Allah.'

Introduction

Perhaps there is no other religion in the history of mankind that has relied so heavily on promotions to support its causes as much as Islam. The religion, which was inaugurated with the words *read, teach and write* in an era when only the privileged were literate, is no stranger to the professional use of promotional means in the propagation of its principles. In fact, the Quran, which can be rightly described as the greatest book that has ever been written on promotions, commands that Muslims acquire and disseminate knowledge:

> *Read in the Name of your Lord Who has created (all that exists). He who has created man from a clot (a piece of thick coagulated blood). Read! And your Lord is the Most Generous. Who has taught (the writing) by the pen. He has taught man that which he knew not.*
>
> Quran 96:1–5

Islam is a religion that is based on dissemination of information and awareness creation, two functions that should be carried out by well-versed and devout adherents through the principle of *Da'waah* (a summons or an invitation), where each Muslim has the role of *Da'eah* (the person making the invitation). The term *Da'waah*, which is central to marketing the religion of Islam, is also known to present-day organizations as promotions, one of the components of the traditional marketing mix, or the 4Ps: product, price, place and promotion.

From day one, and during the period when they were powerless and stateless 14 centuries ago, Muslim holy marketers (those driven by their beliefs to market Islam) perfected and heavily relied on various methods to promote their faith. Using contemporary marketing terms, they excelled in networking and personal selling whereby they generated leads and qualified and contacted prospects, attended gatherings, organized public speeches and debates, utilized public relations and exhibited exemplary role models in their community, and used sales promotions to build and strengthen loyalty among the religion's customer base, i.e., granted special privileges to converts embracing Islam.

Their religious marketing skills and traits proved equally effective in the material marketplace where a smooth transition from the divine to the earthly occurred. The skills that were introduced, inspired and used by the religion to promote religion itself became indispensible to compete in the increasingly globalized world of the Arab merchants; it gave them a 'divine' competitive advantage over other merchants who relied on the traditional marketing wisdom. Islam added and emphasized traits such as kindness, honesty, gradualism, true promises, articulacy, sensitivity to the needs of others, respect for their faiths and ways, a genuine interest in their well-being, and so on. These traits are impossible to adhere to without an extremely strong underlying motive and, indeed, there is no stronger motive than the true believe that paradise is the reward for those who wholeheartedly comply; Islam makes adherence to these and many other traits a worship, without which, ones faith would not be complete.

The Transition of Holy Marketers

Muslims, all of whom are commanded to assume the role of holy marketers according to their own individual capacities, employed the word in its various forms – spoken, sung, implied, lived and written – in order to attract the public to embrace the new faith. Allah's commands to Muslims are clear: 'Let there arise out of you a band of people inviting to all that is good, enjoining what is right, and forbidding what is wrong' Quran (3:104).

The Muslim holy marketers responded with zeal to this and many other similar commands and, as a result, sought to perfect their religious marketing activities using all means available to them. Personalized letters with the logo of the new religion were sent to the emperors of Rome and Persia, virtuous poems were composed replacing the traditional Arab poems saluting wine, women and love and teachers were sent to the tribes, to mention only a few of the numerous promotional activities utilized by devout Muslims in their religious marketing campaigns.

This knowledge, which has been developed to serve the heavenly, was inevitably bound to make a landfall. Many of the holy marketers were also merchants trading either locally in the markets of the Arabian Peninsula, regionally between the Peninsula and the markets of the Fertile Crescent and Egypt, or internationally with the Chinese, Indian, African and European markets. Their abilities were greatly enhanced by the use of their skills as religious marketers and thus they had a significant advantage over other merchants who were not equipped by the skills endorsed by the new teachings. Consumers then, usually unaccustomed to the exhibited magnitude of honesty, kindness, flexibility, generosity and absence of greed, were left with little choice but to embrace the new traders.

The skills of those marketers served them well in both propagating their faith and in making them wealthy. This transformation from the divine into the worldly was done with ease. It did not cause any conflicts or compromises between the two. In fact, such a transformation was clearly encouraged by the teachings of Islam itself where the word *Da'aa* or invited (to embrace) and its

Table 5.1   An approximate guide of some commerce-related words in
              the Quran

The word and its derivatives, using the Arabic root, or the word itself	Frequency, or number of times mentioned in the Quran	The word and its derivatives, using the Arabic root, or the word itself	Frequency, or number of times mentioned in the Quran
Invite (*Da'aa*)	218	Sale (*Ba'aa*)	9
Spend (*Anfaqa*)	72	Usury (*Riba*) (interest rate)	8
Weigh (*Wazana*), weight (*Mizan*), measure (*Kai'l*)	39	Lend (*Aqraza*)	7
Satisfaction (*Razi'a*)	30	Loan (*Qard*)	6
Win (*Faza*)	26	Borrower (*Madeen*)	2
Purchase (*Eshtara*)	25	Competition (*Nafa'sa*)	2
Price (*Thaman*)	11	Market (*Souq*)	2
Product (*Biza'ah*), offer (*Araza*)	11	Delegate (*Fawaza*)	1
Commerce (*Tijara*)	9	Profit (*Rabi'ha*)	1

derivates is repeated more than 218 times in the Quran, as well as countless times in Hadith.

Table 5.1 shows some of the relevant commercial concepts that are mentioned in the Quran and their frequency using the Arabic root word for each concept, or the word itself when the root does not apply. As can be seen in this table, *Da'aa* is the most repeated word and it surpasses by far any other commerce-related word.

Admiring the Power of the 'Word'

In fact, the Quran – the holy book of Islam – could be considered as the greatest book that ever existed on promotions. According to Muslims, its first miracle lies in its style which couldn't be reproduced or imitated even by the Arabs themselves to whom the Quran was revealed in their own tongue. At the time of Mohammad, the Arabs were enchanted by the Arabic language, and it is accepted by Arab historians that their literary talent and eloquence was at its height back then. People used to travel into the desert to write magnificent pieces of poetry, and parents would send their children to stay with Bedouin tribes so that they could learn a purer Arabic than that which was spoken in the cities, in addition to being exposed to less polluted air and a cleaner environment.

Allah challenged these people to produce a literary work of a similar calibre; a new Quran, just one chapter in the Quran, or even just a few verses from it, yet despite all of their eloquence and efforts they failed to match it, even though some of the Quran's short chapters are composed of only a few sentences, called verses.

Celebrating Beauty and Goodness

The Quran teaches that all invitations must be extended with kindness by those who are knowledgeable. 'Invite to the Way of thy Lord with wisdom and beautiful preaching; and argue with them in ways that are best and most gracious' (Quran 16:125). Islam stresses the importance of the use of the words 'beautiful', 'beauty', 'good', 'pardoning', 'council' and 'kindness' in everything a Muslim does. The Prophet teaches: 'Allah is beautiful and He likes beauty', 'Allah is good and He accepts only that which is good', and 'Kindness makes all things beautiful and lack of it makes them ugly'. The Quran attributes the gathering of people around Mohammad due to the fact that he was lenient and gentle:

> Thus it is due to mercy from Allah that you deal with them gently, and had you been rough, hard hearted, they would certainly have dispersed from around you; pardon them therefore and ask pardon for them, and take counsel with them in the affair; so when you have decided, then place your trust in Allah; surely Allah loves those who trust.
>
> Quran 3:159

Cross-cultural Communications

Cultural differences and their effects on the success of promotions are also acknowledged in the Quran. When in discussions with the Christians and the Jews Islam clearly asks its adherents to highlight similarities and avoid all means of arousing animosity, which might ultimately lead to rejection: 'And do not dispute with the followers of the Book except by what is best, except those of them who act unjustly, and say: We believe in that which has been revealed to us and revealed to you, and our Allah and your Allah is One, and to Him do we submit' (Quran 29:46). Finding a common ground between the company and its various markets at the beginning of the relationship improves its chances of success. Because there is always a greater possibility for misunderstanding in cross-cultural communications, Muslims are asked to choose their words carefully: 'Say to My servants that they should (only) say those things that are best' (Quran 17:53).

Gradualism and Persistence

Islam's approach to promotions for societal and other causes stresses the importance of gradualism and persistence. Although Muslim companies, like all other companies in the marketplace, have the right to engage customers and to use and introduce a profoundly different marketing mix, they cannot go around ridiculing the lifestyles and consumption patterns of non-Muslims. The Quran clearly supports a gradual process when introducing concepts that are non-conformist. For example, Islam's strong stance on alcohol is well known even to non-Muslims: its consumption is not allowed under any circumstances. Yet the early Muslims were not suddenly asked to stop drinking wine. Instead, a promotional campaign was gradually implemented over several years leading to a total and successful ban on the product. That campaign should be an exemplary guide to Muslim companies targeting non-Muslim markets, non-Muslim companies targeting Muslim markets or companies introducing new products. It demonstrates the concepts of gradualism, persistence, dissemination of information, comparison and faith as ways of gaining customer acceptance and loyalty. It never shocks and never enters into disputes, it instead, it emphasizes the importance of time in the process of attracting and convincing customers.

First. The extraordinary characteristics of the wine in heaven were described, without mentioning earthly wine. It was left to consumers themselves to make the comparison: 'Round them will be passed a cup of pure wine. White, delicious to the drinkers. Neither will they have *Ghoul* (any kind of hurt, abdominal pain, headache, a sin) from that, nor will they suffer intoxication therefrom' Quran 37:45–7).

Second. Some time later, Muslims were reminded of the many blessings Allah bestowed on them, including the trees from which they produce drinks and consume fruits. As can be seen in the verse, provisions were described as being good while nothing, neither good nor bad, was said about the drink: 'And from the fruits of date-palms and grapes, you derive strong drink and a goodly provision. Verily, therein is indeed a sign for people who have wisdom' (Quran 16:67).

Third. Later, the newly established religion informed its adherents that wine is both bad and good with the word bad preceding the word good, and thus, in accordance with the Arabic writing style, giving it a stronger meaning: 'They ask you (O Muhammad) concerning alcoholic drink and gambling. Say: In them is a great sin, and (some) benefit for men, but the sin of them is greater than their benefit' (Quran 2:219).

Fourth. When the faith of the new adherents strengthened and a more acceptance was anticipated, a stronger command was revealed: 'O you who believe! Approach not the prayer when you are in a drunken state until you know of what you utter' (Quran 4:43).

Finally. When Muslims reached the state of belief where they were willing to do only that which is deemed right by their religion, the final command to prohibit the consumption of alcohol was revealed. No resistance was encountered whatsoever. In fact the few who continued to consume it until then hurried and broke their wine jars and containers in the streets as soon as they heard the command because, by that time, most Muslims had grown to resent wine: 'O you who believe! Intoxicants (all kinds of alcoholic drinks), and gambling, and *Al-Ansâb,* and *Al-Azlâm* (arrows for seeking luck or decision) are an abomination of Satan's work. So avoid (strictly all) that (abomination) in order that you may be successful' (Quran 5:90).

By comparison to the Islamic gradual approach, the compulsory legislative approach that was adopted to ban alcohol in the US in 1933 resulted in the execution of more than 200 alcohol producers, increased the number of alcohol factories from 400 to more than 80,000, and made the product ever more popular across all social and economic classes in the US.

Moreover, Allah has 99 names in Islam; each describing some of His attributes. Muslims are commanded to impersonate as much as they can of each of those Godly attributes, everyone in his/her own capacity. For example, where Allah calls Himself the 'Satisfier of all needs', each Muslim is supposed to endeavour to satisfy the needs of those whom he/she deals with to the best of his/her abilities and to the highest available standards. In much the same way as a teacher is commanded to excel in teaching and a doctor is commanded to treat patients according to the best available knowledge in medicine, a company is commanded to satisfy the needs of its customers in ways that enhance their well-being and prosperity through an enhanced value creation and delivery systems. Those customers, invariably, need to be *informed* and that need has to be satisfied accurately, timely, and with pure intentions; not with the purpose of deception to make gains that would have been otherwise hard to acquire. In much the same way, each of His other names' such as 'the loving', 'the trustee', 'the giver', 'the shaper of beauty', and so on, has clear implications for the various functions of the company.

Finally, for promotions to succeed, all of their components must be credible. Islam places a great deal of emphasis on the importance of honesty and truth in dealings between people. This emphasis is clearly demonstrated in many verses in the Quran and in numerous teachings by the Prophet Mohammad.

Promotions as Promises

At the very core, promotions are promises of hope and fulfilment of desires. These promises are made by sellers in order to attract customers and to encourage them to engage in seemingly mutually beneficial relationships, although it is fair to say that customers might actually be at a disadvantage in many of these relationships. As such, traditional promotions revolve around these three interrelated concepts: (1) promises by sellers, (2) attraction of customers, and (3) mutual benefits. Descriptions of the conventional meaning of these concepts can be found in numerous marketing books and that is why they will not be discussed here. However, what will be discussed is the impact on promotions of a new, fourth concept of *extended accountability*, which is added by Islam.

Extended Accountability

Islam hold both buyers and sellers accountable for their actions not only in front of the Shariah, but more importantly in front of God in this life and in the hereafter. This extension of accountability works as a divine motive for both parties of this relationship to behave responsibly to the best of their knowledge, despite of the deficiency of that knowledge, whom Allah Himself describes as little 'and you are not given aught of knowledge but a little' (Quran 17:85).

The extension also works as a deterrent preventing people from engaging in less than honourable behaviours in business situations. Stating the obvious, some people are not law abiding and they have a tendency to exploit the system or bend the rules. To quote Plato: 'Good people do not need laws to tell them to act responsibly, while bad people will find a way around the laws.' Laws are adopted by good people but enforced on others. However, since some people are willing and able to break these laws without being detected by the human legal systems, they are constantly reminded that their actions are monitored by the One who 'hears the sound of the footsteps of the black ant on the deaf rock at the dark night' (Prophet Mohammad). One can indeed escape being observed by humans, but one cannot dodge divine observation. Therefore, since the laws of this world don't represent a valid disincentive to some, the warning of an exact and just ruling in the hereafter when the time for repentance has already passed represents an added control on undesired behaviour. Still, though, it is important to make another obvious statement here: a non-believer is certainly exempt from this deterrent simply because they don't believe that such a time – the hereafter – will be.

The extended accountability dimension profoundly affects the execution of the three dimensions of promotions, i.e., promises, attractions and benefits, since it forces marketers to see them from an entirely new perspective, as will be demonstrated in the following sections.

Extended Accountability and Sellers' Promises

A promise is 'an undertaking or assurance given by one person to another agreeing or guaranteeing to do or give something, or not to do or give something, in the future' (Thefreedictionary 2011). Companies, in their efforts to compete, seek to attract customers through making promises that are sometimes hard to fulfil and sometimes even without any real intention of fulfilling them. These companies can make customers' follow-up on promises, customer complaints and customer queries extremely difficult to the point where customers question the feasibility of any action they might undertake to get companies to deliver on their promises. Fine prints, misleading advertising, confusing terms and conditions and the referral of responsibility for fulfilment to other parties are among the numerous ways that companies can utilize to dissipate the perceptions created by their own deliberate campaigns about the nature of their commitments. As a result, customers are left disgruntled and frequently powerless to do much other than to forget that it happened at all and move on. Cases against sellers may take up to several years in courts and thus can harshly disrupt an angry customer's life's rhythm. Only customers with great stamina and perseverance are willing to go along that road. Most customers will choose either to do nothing or to simply switch suppliers.

The Islamic standpoint on promises is unswerving; promises have to be fulfilled, otherwise they should not be made in the first place. The Prophet said,

> *Whoever has the following four (characteristics) will be a pure hypocrite and whoever has one of the following four characteristics will have one characteristic of hypocrisy unless and until he gives it up.*

> *1. Whenever he is entrusted, he betrays.*

> *2. Whenever he speaks, he tells a lie.*

> *3. Whenever he makes a covenant, he proves treacherous.*

> *4. Whenever he quarrels, he behaves in a very imprudent, evil and insulting manner.*

Allah, before he asks people to honour their promises, declares to them that He '… will not fail His promise, but most people do not know' (Quran 30:6). Allah also commends his apostles as truthful: 'And mention Ismail in the Book; surely he was truthful in (his) promise' (Quran 19:54). Allah describes himself as One who doesn't fail a promise and He praises his apostles as truthful, and concludes by asking the rest of the people to follow suit. For example, He states that it is not enough for Muslims to face Mecca and pray, being a Muslim is certainly more than directions and places:

> *righteousness is this that one should believe in Allah and the last day and the angels and the Book and the prophets, and give away wealth out of love for Him to the near of kin and the orphans and the needy and the wayfarer and the beggars and for (the emancipation of) the captives, and keep up prayer and pay the poor-rate; and the performers of their promise when they make a promise, and the patient in distress*

and affliction and in time of conflicts-- these are they who are true (to
themselves) and these are they who guard (against evil).

Quran 2:177

The word 'promise' is deeply ingrained in Muslims' psyches, regardless of how religiously observant they are. The above-quoted Hadith about hypocrites is one of the best known among Muslims and it is commonly used in normal conversations. Arab and Islamic histories are also filled with proverbs and stories about the importance of fulfilling promises. For example, the pre-Islamic Arab Arqoob, who lived in an unspecified time BC according to Arab historians, remains until this day an example of a person who failed to keep his promises. Almost every man and woman in the Arab world knows the story. Arqoob had a farm of palm trees. A poor man came asking him for charity. Arqoob told him that it was not the time of dates and that he should return when the crop sweetened. The man returned as promised but he was told that he should go now and come back when the crop softened. When he returned again, he was told to return when the crop ripened. The man, having no choice, went away and returned at the designated time to take his promised dates. By that time, Arqoob had already collected the dates and stored them. Only then did the poor man recognize that he was being lied to and that Arqoob was only buying time.

As discussed above, marketers must be able to demonstrate that they are honest, intend to deliver on their promises, that their promises are realistic and that what is being offered is Shariah-compliant. A Shariah-compliant offer is one that fulfils the following conditions:

1.   The good or service on offer must in itself be *Halal* (see Chapter 3 for a deeper understanding of *Halal* products).

2.   It must be delivered through a *Halal* supply chain.

3.   If a salesperson knows that the product is being bought for purposes that are not permissible under Shariah then that salesperson is religiously held accountable not only for selling it but sometimes for advertising it in the first place.

4.   It must be advertised using Shariah-compliant means.

5.   Customers must be fully informed of what they are buying; nothing that could affect their decision is to be concealed from them. Total transparency must be strictly adhered to; if a seller has something to hide then he shouldn't be trading.

General Implications for Businesses

Islam does not tolerate deceptive promotional behaviours. It clearly denounces all kinds of false assertion, unfounded accusation, concoction and false testimony (Quran 43:19). Thus, it is unethical for a sales organization to over-praise its products or to attribute to them non-existent qualities. Within the Islamic ethical framework, creating false impressions as a means to promote an offering is prohibited. In general, this framework is built on several rules including (Chachi and Latiff 2008):

1.   Rejection of high-pressure manipulations or misleading sales tactics. To use models with pretty hair to give the impression that their hair is looking good because of the shampoo they are advertising is deception according to Islam. Such promotional campaigns drive some women to go to extremes to have hair like that in the adverts. Many other women are made to feel bad about themselves because they know they will never have hair that looks like the hair in these adverts. Exploiting the basic instinct of consumers with a view to gain profits and greater market share is not an activity a Muslim marketer will engage in.

2.   Avoidance of sales promotions that use deception. To use healthy children in advertisement directed at other children when promoting potentially harmful products such as fast foods, fizzy drinks, unhealthy snacks and other products to give the false impression that their good health is a result of consuming these products, or to hint to unsuspecting parents that allowing kids to consume them is good parenting, is *Haram*. The truth and nothing but the truth is the first commandment of Islamic promotions.

3.   Avoidance of promoting products that are considered *Haram*. There is no such thing as an Islamic promotion for alcohol, pork, sex, music, narcotics or intoxicants.

4.   Avoidance of using certain appeals such as sexual, emotional, fear, and so on. For example, the common practice of using women in swimsuits to promote cars in car shows in Western culture is totally denounced in Islam.

5.   Advocating consumption as a form of worship. Muslims are commanded to show that Allah has provided them. Muslims are ordered to look their best wherever and whenever possible. Adhering to this command is considered a good deed. 'Allah loves to see the signs of His blessings on his servant' (Hadith).

6.   Avoidance of the provocation of desires and acknowledging that certain desires will never be fulfilled regardless of one's wealth. 'If the son of Adam had money equal to a valley, then he will wish for another similar to it, for nothing can satisfy the eye of Adam's son except dust. And Allah forgives him who repents to Him' (Hadith).

7.   Advocating moderation in consumption. Promotions must not encourage extravagance or over-consumption. 'Food for one is enough for two and food for two is enough for four' (Hadith).

8.   Disclosure and transparency. A customer must be informed of what is getting. Marketers must disclose all faults in their goods, whether obvious or hidden. Acting otherwise is to act fraudulently. All known defects which cannot be seen and cannot be found out by the purchaser must be disclosed. Only true documents which reveal accurate specifications will exchange hands.

9.   Avoidance of promotions that could lead to the long-term mental of physical deterioration or contribute to the dullness of the mind.

10.   Excessive use of fantasy, the use of suggestive language and behaviour and stereotyping of women in advertising as objects to lure and attract customers are all activities that a Muslim marketer will avoid.

Implications for Advertising

1.   Use males, not females.

2.   Use cartoons and animations, not humans.

3.   Use natural objects such as landscapes, animals, birds, and so on, not humans.

4.   Use conforming backgrounds, not rebellious ones.

5.   Use quiet Islamic music, not loud Western music. No rock and roll and no rap.

6.   Use optimistic music and settings, no blues.

7.   Make no reference to sexuality, nudity, indulgence, hatred or racism.

8.   Utilize Islamic TV and radio channels, not the all-dancing all-singing ones.

9.   Emphasize modesty and respect.

10. Use green and white, avoid black and blue. Black is associated with mourning, darkness and loss of guidance while blue is described as the colour of the wrongdoers in the Day of Judgement.

Implications for Sales Promotions

1.   The person offering the promotions should be recognized as a Muslim, especially in the case of food items.

2.   Muslims go shopping in families so make sure to give to all not just some of the family members. Especially when it is a taste promotion.

3.   Have a promotion after prayers, not before. Muslims usually avoid eating immediately before prayers because Islam encourages them

to clean their teeth each time they pray. Moreover, they are usually rushing to mosques and thus do not have enough time to taste.

4.   Muslims are becoming increasingly sceptical about the motivations underlying the 'buy one, get one free' and other similar offers citing reasons as low quality, impending expiry dates, poor warehousing conditions, and so on. Marketers need to make sure that their products are as good as any others that are not on sale.

5.   Local families in the Arabian Gulf countries go shopping in the morning because markets are less crowded and because women in these families are usually unemployed. They are often well-off and hence not interested in getting jobs. The morning is the best time for them to go shopping since their children will be at school. Families of other Arab countries go either during weekends or in the evening. This is so because many mothers in non-Arab Gulf families work and the only time the family can get together is in the evening. A marketer must know when and how to appeal to both.

6.   A sales promotion must be seen as a gift, not as a charity or as a way of luring in customers. Muslim consumers are wary of seemingly free offers and many of them also refuse to take charity. Although Islam encourages everyone to give in charity, it strongly asks people to support themselves and not rely on others. Many Muslims will reject a trail straight away if they are not sure about it.

7.   Muslim populations in general are very colourful and they like colours and celebrations. Promotions must be presented in a family-friendly atmosphere of celebrations.

Implications for Telemarketing

1.   When calling at homes, employ women, not men. Arab and Muslim men in general are very sensitive to women in their families talking to strangers, even if it is on a business-related matter.

2.   If they say no, do not call again unless you have something that is genuinely different. Marketers who follow the policy of 'Knock and

You Shall Receive' will soon find the police knocking on their own doors, in addition to getting an immediate unsympathetic response.

3.   Do not call between *Zuhur* (noon) and *Asr* (afternoon) prayers. Muslims in many countries have a habit of napping within that time period.

Implications for Public Relations

1.   Celebrate real people and avoid showbiz celebrities. Although many Muslims can hardly be described as observant, the majority are not into showbiz. Do not be fooled by the noise made by the huge number of satellite TV stations in the Muslim world, they live in their own wonderland. Showbiz – especially if women are involved – is considered in many Muslim cultures as a domain for a particular social class that doesn't gain much respect within the society as a whole. Involving them in activities might create some commotion, but it portrays the company as disrespectful of the religion and the culture.

2.   The people involved in the activity must be from the local population, dressing, talking and behaving like them. There are many implied local rules of behaviour which an outsider could easily miss and thus turn the public relations event into a disaster instead of a success.

3.   Being charitable is greatly glorified in Islam. A company that is seen to be genuinely engaged in voluntary and real charitable activities will win the hearts of the Muslim consumers who are reminded several times a day in their prayers about the importance of alms, donations and other forms of selfless acts.

Conclusion

Islamic business ethics imply that accurate product information should be provided when a good is sold as well as in the associated advertising and marketing literature. Advertisements should not offend Islamic values. For example, the use of scantily dressed women for product promotion would certainly be regarded as unacceptable. Television commercials in Muslim countries often depict consumers in a respectable family environment (Wilson 2006).

Islam takes a strong stand on both the content and the delivery of promotions. The philosophy of 'ends justify means' is strongly denounced since both ends and means must be Shariah-compliant. According to the teachings of Islam, increasing sales does not justify using the meaningless 'Everyday Low Sales'. Attracting more customers is not a justification for the exploitation of women as objects in advertising campaigns. The Islamic rule is very clear in this regard: selling now at a price which the society has to pay later is considered ruination, the punishment for which could be as severe as death. Islamic promotions mean promoting only what pleases God through equally pleasing methods, i.e., what is being advertised must be entirely *Halal*, promoted via *Halal* channels, by *Halal* companies using *Halal* promotional materials. For example, if a company uses leaflets as part of a promotional campaign it will achieve more success if it makes its Muslim customers aware that the paper used in the campaign is recycled or recyclable and that trees were planted to replace those that were used to manufacture the paper. This is so because the tree and greenery command special respect and admiration in Islam; all early Islamic military campaigns were instructed by the Prophet and by his successors 'not to cut a tree'. Equally true, seeking to employ an advertising agency that is all Shariah-compliant to promote content that is not so compliant, will not work either.

To conclude, promotions can be seen as a channel beginning with a *Halal* product produced by an honest, compassionate and knowledgeable manufacturer and ending with a customer with good intentions. If the advertising agency knew or suspected that the manufacturer's operations, processes, ingredients, etc. are not compliant, or if customers intend to use the product inappropriately, it becomes a sin to promote for that particular manufacture or target that particular customer segment.

Key Terms:

- Islamic promotions
- Holy marketers
- Promotions as promises
- Sellers' promises
- Misleading sales tactics
- Extended accountability
- Consumer boycott
- *Da'waah*
- The power of the word
- Cross-cultural communications
- Gradualism and persistence.

References

Chachi, A. H. A. and S. A. Latiff. (2008). 'Islamic marketing ethics and its impact on customer satisfaction in the Islamic banking industry.' *Journal of Islamic Economics* 2(1): 23–40.

Thefreedictionary (2011). 'Promise.' Retrieved 11 February 2011 from: http://www.thefreedictionary.com/promise.

Jury, Louise. (1997). 'Nike to trash trainers that offended Islam.' *Independent*, 25 June.

Wilson, R. (2006). 'Islam and business.' *Thunderbird International Business Review* 48(1): 109–23.

6

Islamic Logistics *(Halal* Logistics)

Making your whole operation Halal is actually the most cost-efficient method of production. It would almost be easier if all suppliers did things that way.

Meat suppliers will eventually become totally Halal since it makes sense to streamline their operations and ensure abattoirs are operating according to the Halal principles.

Bin Hendi, hospitality executive chief, in Taylor 2009

Learning Objectives

After reading this chapter, you should be able to:

- Understand the concept of *Halal* integrity
- Describe the growing importance of Islamic logistics
- Understand the definition and requirements of Islamic logistics
- Understand the contribution of Islamic logistics to firms' competitive advantage
- Understand the contribution of Islamic ports and *Halal* hubs to Islamic logistics.

Maintaining *Halal* Integrity in *Al Islami*

Recognized as one of the top 40 Arab brands by Forbes magazine, Al Islami foods is a regional *Halal* brand, a private company based in the UAE (United Arab Emirates) and a top Middle Eastern food producer that has been operating in the *Halal* industry since 1981. The company's pursuit of its mission of raising the profile and standard of *Halal* food helped it get many awards including the *Best Halal Food* award given by the UAE's Superbrands Council at the 2010 inaugural Gulfood Awards. The company was also voted a *Super Brand* in the UAE in the same year.

Al Islami's business is being continuously diversified as the company enters into new businesses building on its strength in the food industry. Its portfolio currently includes several well-known names such as Al Islami Foods International, Al Islami Foods UAE, the fast-food restaurant chain Al Farooj Fresh, the food kiosk Al Islami Cart and Al Islami Meat Shops where customers can find fresh chicken, mutton, lamb and beef. The company also has a dry food product line where Al Islami tuna, beans, honey and dates are sold (Mansoor 2010).

In addition to being one of the first *Halal* brands in the Muslim world, Al Islami's success is attributed to other factors such as its innovation in the *Halal* food industry, strict quality assurance and world-class supply chain and resources that allow it to maintain the *Halal* integrity and *Halal* branding of its operations.

In particular, the company gives special attention to process supervision over its supply chains in order to maintain the *Halal* integrity of its products. The company monitors and controls the entire supply chain processes starting from production, storage and transportation, to supervising local suppliers where products are sourced. According to Hasan Rimawi, chief technical officer at Al Islami Foods, the company's approach to Halalization includes a *Halal* supply chain that spans 'everything from the procurement and preparation of genuine *Halal* ingredients to the manufacturing and delivery of the final product all the way to customer shelves.' Such an approach to *Halal* assurance means that strong relationships needed to be forged with channel partners to ensure that each product is manufactured to the highest quality standards and is not mixed with any non-*Halal* ingredients, such as alcoholic or pork-related products, throughout the entire chain. This also includes taking suitable measures in other areas of the logistics process, such as transporting *Halal*-fed animals to slaughterhouses or when shipping chilled or frozen *Halal* meat in enclosed shipping containers (Khan 2009).

Introduction

Many countries in the world, both Muslim and non-Muslim, are making substantial investments to become regional *Halal* hubs that provide special manufacturing centres as well as systems for *Halal* logistics in order to maintain product purity during shipping and storage. These *Halal* market-supply chains are changing manufacturing in many countries, most of which are non-Muslim. For example, Brazilian suppliers have built *Halal* chicken-slaughtering facilities to cater to the needs of Islamic countries such as Saudia Arabia. New Zealand, the world's biggest exporter of *Halal* lamb, continues to host delegations from Muslim countries to ensure the *Halal* integrity of its exports to Islamic markets. The Netherlands, through its *Halal* hub in Rotterdam port, has built *Halal* warehouses so that imported *Halal* goods are stored away from *Haram* products such as pork or alcohol. By expanding its connections to the *Halal* hubs in Malaysia, the Netherlands is planning to maximize Rotterdam's role as Europe's biggest port. Domino's Pizza now sources *Halal* pepperoni from Malaysia for its *Halal* pizzas. Finally, a hypermarket run by the French Carrefour at the Mid Valley Megamall in Kuala Lumpur implements a very elaborate *Halal* process to keep *Halal* foods separate. In that hypermarket, goods that divide Islamic scholars on whether they are *Halal* or *Haram* are coded with green stickers to alert customers to their Shariah-compliance status. Clearly *Haram* goods such as those containing alcohol, pork or tobacco are isolated in a glass room at the back of the store, hidden away from the majority of the store's customers. Further, these *Haram* products are handled by staff wearing designated blue gloves and sealed in airtight pink plastic wrapping after purchase, in order to avoid contaminating the main store (Power and Abdullah 2009).

It is important to understand that the *Halal* industry no longer stops at production. Shipping and storage companies from Malaysia to Rotterdam are positioning themselves as champions in *Halal* logistics. For example, Malaysia's national shipping company's (MISC) weekly Halal Express Service is a liner launched to carry *Halal* beef from Australia and New Zealand to the Middle East and sometimes beyond. The company also operates a *Halal* logistics hub near Kuala Lumpur, which has cold-storage facilities, sterilization units and a lab to test products to ensure they are *Halal* (Power and Gatsiounis 2007).

Halal Logistics as Source of Competitive Advantage

As explained throughout this book, the concept of *Halal* is much broader than commonly understood. Traditionally, what has been considered to determine whether a product is *Halal* or not was the final stages of production where the process and ingredients are ensured to be compliant with the principles of Islamic Shariah; not much attention was paid to the supply chain as a whole. In reality the concept of *Halal* extends much further to include the entire product logistics.

> *Halal supply chains include everything from the procurement and preparation of genuine Halal ingredients to the manufacturing and delivery of the final product all the way to customer shelves. This includes the separation of Halal ingredients or finished products from non Halal products, such as alcoholic or pork-related products, throughout the entire chain.*
>
> *Khan 2009*

This long chain of activities preceding the final step and the activities following consumption is usually overlooked and thus a product might end up being classified as *Halal* despite being moved through a *Haram* channel. This short-sightedness in defining *Halal* is being corrected now as accreditation authorities, governments and businesses come to realize that such an extension of the activities considered does actually represent an advantage to be had, not a burden to be avoided.

Companies that can demonstrate that their *Halal* product has actually been prepared, transported and delivered through a *Halal* supply chain will clearly be at an advantage over other companies who stop short of this or are unable to use their supply chains as leverage for the promotion of their *Halal* products.

Because the final *Halal* product is usually the subject of traditional promotions to Muslim consumers, going beyond that point and showing that the entire process is also *Halal* will undoubtedly relieve some of the doubts of the suspicious Muslim consumer who is under continuous bombardment from young Internet-savvy Muslims who are willing to declare and denounce a product as *Haram* based on blogs and hearsay rather than on actual facts. The widespread influence of these groups, more driven by deep religious zealousness than accurate religious knowledge, comes from their large numbers and relentless efforts to scrutinize. Therefore, it is in the long-term interest of businesses dealing with this emotional and religious Muslim market led by its young to build a documented reputation that the various stages leading to the final production and delivery of the product are Shariah-compliant.

Communicating the fact that a company's entire logistics are compliant might even be more important than declaring that the final product is *Halal*, which is usually no more than stating the obvious since such a product would not be targeted at Muslim consumers if was *Haram* in the first place. Although the extension of the contents of marketing campaigns are still at an early stage, some companies have already began utilizing some of their logistical activities as a differentiating factor that sets them apart from other players in the *Halal* market. For example some TV advertisements targeting Muslims now include short videos of clean factories, well-dressed workers, sunny green fields, and 'happy' farm animals transported in cruise-like ships or flown in business class.

Although the use of logistics as a source of competitive advantage remains in its infancy as far as the Islamic market is concerned, it is already making a difference in the way marketing campaigns are being carried out; it is acting as an eye-opener in the field. Other companies who have not done so yet will have no option but to follow suit and thus force an upgrade in the use of logistics as a key ingredient in the near-future marketing practice of companies targeting the Muslim consumer. These companies are already realizing that *Halal* is losing its position as a core selling concept because all competitors in the market are operating under its banner and thus making it a core requirement rather than a differentiating factor.

Halal Hubs and *Halal* Logistics

Governments around the world are increasingly realizing the importance of *Halal* logistics to the establishment of a *Halal* industry that can compete successfully within the sophisticated *Halal* market. Some of these governments are investing substantially to create what is called *Halal* hubs where tailor-made manufacturing centres and *Halal* logistics ensure that product purity is maintained during shipping, handling and storage. So far, the most influential players in the field of Islamic or *Halal* logistics are Brazil, New Zealand and the Netherlands – obviously the three are not countries with dominant Muslim populations.

Some Muslim countries are also strengthening their capabilities and developing *Halal* logistics, mainly Malaysia, Dubai and Turkey. The advantage provided by the location of these countries allows them to link the regions where the bulk of the *Halal* industry is concentrated: South East Asia and Australia, the Middle East and Europe. While Malaysia builds on its well-developed *Halal* certification standards, emerging *Halal* logistics and proximity to Australia and New Zealand, Dubai's advantage lies in its massive shipping abilities and its central location as a link between East and West. Turkey on the other hand, is building on its potential to be a major centre for the development of *Halal* industry drawing on its proximity to Europe as well as its newly discovered political role among Muslim nations.

While the European Union (EU) is already working on a project that would allow the issue of certificates for *Halal* food, the Organization of the Islamic Conference (OIC), which is composed of more than 50 mostly Islamic states, is determined to extend its umbrella over the *Halal* industry within the Muslim world – that is, before Europe can make further gains in the field. Although the OIC's perspective on ensuring dominance over the *Halal* industry as a whole seems legitimate from a purely business justification, it nonetheless contradicts Islam's own view which commands that a job should be performed by the one who can do it best. If Europeans can excel in the development of *Halal* logistics then they should be allowed to do so and no efforts should be made to undermine them. In Islamic economics the development of *Halal* logistics is better for the world and therefore it doesn't matter much who develops it. Of course it would be more in line with the faith if Muslims did that first; that is, if they are to do that. Otherwise, the progress towards *Halal* logistics should not be delayed because of a dispute over who should be leading it.

Halal Ports

A central theme in *Halal* logistics is the establishment of *Halal* ports where *Halal* support services are provided. Of these ports two are taking the central stage at the field of Islamic or *Halal* logistics; Rotterdam Port and Penang Port.

ROTTERDAM PORT

Aiming to become the port of entry for *Halal* goods into the EU and working together with other market parties such as Hecny group, Eurofrigo, and Vat Logistics, the port of Rotterdam offers *Halal* supply chain solutions and dedicated *Halal* warehousing and a distribution zone in the Netherlands. The port authority has also commissioned the Halal Audit Company (HAC) to draw up a *Halal* logistics handbook. The port was first officially recognized as *Halal* in 2009 and a *Halal* certificate was awarded. The certification made Rotterdam the first European port where products are handled and distributed according to Islamic laws. The port has nonetheless been working since 2006 to become a distribution centre for *Halal* products imported into the European market from Indonesia and Malaysia.

PENANG PORT

Following on the footsteps of Rotterdam port, Penang port is preparing itself to be the top *Halal* business hub in Asia. The Penang State Government established an agency named Penang International Halal Hub (PIHH) to oversee the coordination, facilitation, promotion and development of *Halal* industries in the state of Penang in Malaysia. The agency is to be positioned as a link between investors, suppliers and the global *Halal* market.

Penang Port, which is progressively being expanded into a mainly *Halal* port, following the demand for *Halal* shipments, takes advantage of the opportunities provided by the *Halal* industry in southern Thailand, which is currently exporting through Bangkok, an aspirant *Halal* hub itself. The port is also planning to tap into the larger *Halal* growth triangle encompassing Indonesia, Malaysia and Thailand.

The *Halal* port in Penang, which is similar to Rotterdam's *Halal* port, has cold-room facilities, storage areas and other related facilities to store and handle *Halal* products. Both ports are developing standard operating procedures, promoting a so called 'Halal Super Highway', and engaged in projects on *Halal* shipments between Malaysia and the Netherlands. They are also establishing a direct liner service between both countries.

Requirements of *Halal* Logistics

According to Marco Tieman, chief executive officer of LBB Teams, 'Halal logistics can be defined as the process of managing the procurement, movement, storage and handling of materials, parts, livestock and semi-finished inventory, both food and non-food, through the organization and the supply chain in compliance with the principles of the Shariah law' (2009). As such, the *Halal* logistics system involves the organization and provision of integrated and value-added services to the *Halal* industry. The core components of this system include the services of transportation, warehousing, storage, cold rooms, containerization, packaging, test labs, traceability, networking infrastructure, Islamic financial services and marketing. These components need to fulfil two main requirements: ensuring actual and perceptual Shariah-compliance. They must prevent actual contamination as well as provide assurance to consumers that the entire line of services is *Halal* or, in other words, maintain the *Halal* integrity of a product.

More specifically, the key to a Shariah-compliant supply chain is the separation of *Halal* from *Haram* products to avoid cross-contamination and shipping mistakes, and to ensure consistency with the expectations and perceptions of Muslim consumers. If a so-called *Halal* supply chain does not support such a separation, *Halal* and *Haram* products could mix together at any of its value-adding stages. Like all other chains, the performance of the *Halal* supply chain is only as good as its weakest link.

Requirements of *Halal* Logistics

THE PREVENTION OF ACTUAL CONTAMINATION

Halal logistics providers should ensure the prevention of: (1) cross-contamination that could result from shared facilities and handling, and (2) contamination from residuals and traces such as aromas, which could result from shared use and inefficient cleaning. This condition can be achieved through having a dedicated transportation service that transports nothing but *Halal* products and entirely separate warehousing, storage and cold-room facilities where only *Halal* products are stored and handled. Furthermore, the containerization and packaging operations should also be handled in dedicated facilities by separate equipment and workers. However, if it is not at all possible to employ a separate workforce to carry out these *Halal* activities then special care must be given to workers' hygiene. This includes the use of different and distinguishable uniforms for handling *Halal* and placing restrictions on the movement of workers and machines and tools between *Halal* and *Haram* premises and operations.

ASSURANCE TO CONSUMERS

The *Halal* logistics facilities discussed above are not sufficient themselves to create the perception of *Halal* logistical operations; they need to be augmented by a multitude of other related services. These include:

1.   Providing easy access to advanced test labs that can give accurate and speedy results on the type and permissibility of all of the ingredients, both declared and hidden, that are used in the manufacturing of the product. An important element in here is that of forging linkages with *Halal* research centres around the world to allow investors to leverage on for product and process innovation and improvement.

2.   Preparing records that show all activities and stages of product manufacturing, handling, and movement and making these records available to both public and private businesses and consumers. These records should allow comprehensive product traceability – consumers and other interested parties would be able to trace the product back to a very early stage in its production and to reveal its individual ingredients. Providers of *Halal* logistics will also need to create awareness among exporters on the hub's *Halal* facilities to enable them to trace where the raw materials were obtained from, their packaging, and the company used to transport the products. These can provide enhanced traceability and link to the global market.

3.   Building an enhanced networking infrastructure that assists companies in organizing networks of suppliers and manufacturers, where involved businesses and consumers can source high-quality *Halal* ingredients and raw materials and form relations that ease the conduct of their *Halal* business and allow them to engage in more profitable operations. In addition to databases on *Halal* providers and consumers which enable both businesses and consumers can locate each others, *Halal* logistics providers need to provide or be in close proximity to supporting facilities such as mosques, Islamic hotel and catering services and gender-based sports and other facilities.

Providing Islamic financial services that cater specifically to the needs of the parties involved in *Halal* logistics would indeed add to the image of the *Halal* supply chain and the product involved as being Shariah-compliant. Islamic banking, insurance and financial services should be available to the *Halal* logistics partners, in addition to the availability of international financial institutions and offshore banking facilities.

Finally, in marketing *Halal* logistics it is important not to ignore the psychological dimension wherein a *Halal* product is an extended concept, not just the core and final product, be it a loaf of bread or a glass of milk. So far, most marketing campaigns targeting the Muslim consumer seem to neglect this dimension which is gaining an ever increasing importance since the word *Halal* alone is being overused by sellers to promote their products. *Halal* as a description is no longer the distinguishing factor it used to be, at least not among Muslim consumers.

Conclusion

Sellers are coming to realize that carrying non-*Halal* items on their shelves limits their market reach since Muslims will be discouraged from dealing with them. In addition, offering both *Haram* and *Halal* products will result in extra costs because separate facilities and operations need to be organized. Going *Halal*, nonetheless, is not as straightforward or as easy as it might seem because:

> *The complexities of the Halal supply chain extend much further than the usual concerns regarding unbroken cool chains and the efficient delivery of fresh food produce. To be at the top of the Halal logistics game, players need to be well versed in the whole ethos in order to maintain what is known as the 'Halal integrity' of a food product.*
>
> *Khan 2009*

Overcoming these complexities and engaging with *Halal*, although challenging, represents an unprecedented opportunity for companies looking for growth prospects outside their traditional markets, which are losing their appeal due mainly to saturation and maturity.

Undoubtedly, *Halal* logistics will be the playgrounds where future winners and losers will be determined. The activities that comprise *Halal* logistics are numerous and thus have the potential to provide ambitious players in the field with ample opportunities to differentiate themselves and stand out from the crowds scrambling to snatch a piece of this vast market. These activities begin even before ploughing the earth and continue through to actual consumption and recycling. Indeed, a competitive advantage can be built around each single activity along a company's supply chain; it is here where battles over the dominance of Islamic markets will be fought so companies must be prepared.

Key Terms:

- *Halal* integrity
- Islamic logistics
- *Halal* logistics
- *Halal* supply chains
- Shariah-compliant supply chain
- Procurement
- Value-added services
- Traceability
- Cross-contamination
- High-quality *Halal* ingredients
- Competitive advantage
- Islamic ports
- *Halal* hubs.

References

Air Cargo World (2009). 'Hard look at Halal.' *Air Cargo World* 99: 18.

Khan, N. (2009). 'Special report: Halal logistics.' 30 July. Retrieved from http://www.arabiansupplychain.com/article-385-special-report-halal-logistics/1/print/#show=comments.

Mansoor, Z. (2010). 'Al Islami Foods – taking "Halal" to new heights.' *Dinarstandard* June. Retrieved 13 August 2010 from http://www.dinarstandard.com/index.html.

Power, C. and S. Abdullah (2009). 'Buying Muslim.' *Time South Pacific* (Australia/New Zealand edition) 173(20): 31–4.

Power, C. and I. Gatsiounis (2007). 'Meeting the Halal test.' *Forbes* 179(8): 82–5.

Taylor, L. (2009). 'The Halal revolution.' *Arabian Business*, 10 July.

PART 3

Issues in Islamic Marketing

7

Muslim Consumer Behaviour

O Children of Adam! Take your adornment (by wearing your clean clothes), while praying and going round (the Tawâf of) the Ka'bah, and eat and drink but waste not by extravagance, certainly He (Allâh) likes not Al-Musrifûn (those who waste by extravagance).

Quran 7:31

Learning Objectives

After reading this chapter, you should be able to understand:

- Who Muslim consumers are
- The motivations underlying their consumption choices
- What, when and how they consume
- The effect of the country of origin on their consumption choices
- Common demographic attributes among world Muslim populations.

Introduction

In an Islamic market, religious teachings clearly influence the choices of Muslims. For example, the concept of *Halal* (comparable to Kosher in Judaism) affects every single aspect of a Muslim's life; it affects the decisions of what to buy and what to sell; the terms, time and place of the sale; the promotional activities and with whom to transact. It also affects margins, mark-ups and ingredients. These activities are also subject to the central Islamic concept of 'no harm' which forbids all exchanges, activities, and transactions that cause harm to the earth or any of its occupants, including humans, trees and animals, seas and oceans, and land and air. An exchange that is perceived to be in violation of these or any of the other numerous detailed Islamic principles is likely to face major obstacles in a Muslim market that is increasingly becoming aware of the values dictated by its religion.

The study of the Muslim consumers' behaviour is an area of interest that is gradually becoming the focus of academic and business professionals. While academics' efforts are driven mainly by the appeal of pioneering scientific achievements, business professionals' inquiries are more practical in nature and aim at helping businesses connect effectively with their Muslim consumer base.

In turn, Muslims, whose consumption is a key element in the formation of their identity, are becoming even more aware and observant of the requirements of their religion and thus creating complex challenges for international marketers who are used to neglecting religion in their marketing campaigns. The change brought by this awareness is influencing Muslims economic decisions and forcing marketers targeting them to play by new rules and often in new unfamiliar playgrounds that are characterized by transformed world markets, new advertising strategies and religious instead of rational consumer behaviour.

To help marketers deal with the challenges posed by the distinct nature of the Muslim consumer and to assist them in their efforts to understand and connect with the Islamic markets, this chapter introduces and discusses, in detail, various key factors that affect the behaviour of the Muslim consumer. For example, the term 'Muslim consumers' is defined, motivations underlying their consumption decisions are clarified, answers to the questions of what, when and how do they consume are provided, their attitudes concerning country of origin and its effect on their decisions are explained, and shared demographic attributes among the world Muslim populations are presented.

Who is the Muslim Consumer?

The Islamic market is composed of Muslim and non-Muslim consumers – please refer to Chapter 2 for details on Islamic markets. These two distinct categories of consumers differ significantly on several issues such as size, location, motives, buying behaviour and consumption patterns. A clear distinction between them is necessary for planning and executing the firm's marketing strategy in the Islamic market.

The definition of the Muslim consumer is not as straight forward as it might seem. Being a Muslim by birth does not necessarily signify that a person does actually search for, adopt or consume products that are Shariah-compliant. It is a well-known fact that some Muslims consume alcohol, dine at restaurants that don't serve *Halal* food and arrange their finances through conventional rather than Islamic banking. Nonetheless, while the weakened conventional banks have survived so far and continue to this day to provide their services to a diminishing segment of non-observing Muslims, it is very difficult to find *Haram* fast-moving consumer goods (FMCGs) on supermarket shelves within a Muslim community. However, if they are found, those who consume them tend not to go public about it due to the massive cultural pressures against their use, which could harm their reputation within the community and in many cases lead to social rejection. It is a very common practice in Arab societies for women to refuse to marry men who are known to drink alcohol, entertain at night clubs or work in conventional banks.

CULTURE-COMPLIANT MUSLIMS

Consuming non-Shariah-compliant products is a complicated and serious concern to those Muslims who consume them, due to the stigma that surrounds the consumption of these products. To illustrate, Muslims who drink alcoholic beverages tend to be very secretive about that fact and go to great lengths to avoid being detected by the society. A common behaviour in wine consumption among its Muslim consumer base is to buy it from stores at times during the day or the week when the market is least crowded, use unmarked bags and boxes to conceal it, and remain seated in their cars behind tinted glass, wearing large black sunglasses that cover much of the face and waiting for the delivery person to bring the wine to the car. When a person consumes alcohol sometimes even his own family doesn't know about it, unless that person gets too deep into alcohol consumption and no efforts to conceal it will do any good. This kind of a consumer can be called a culture-compliant rather than a Shariah-compliant Muslim because their main concern in consumption is how they will be looked at by their society, not the violation of the teachings of their religion. The non-Shariah-compliant products they seek are hard to find in an Islamic society anyway.

SHARIAH-COMPLIANT MUSLIMS

Shariah-compliant Muslims are those Muslims who are aware of the teachings of the religion of Islam relating to what to consume, what not to consume, how to consume it and when and where to consume it and they mostly adhere to these teachings. They represent the vast majority of Muslims worldwide, both in Islamic countries and in non-Islamic countries, and the products they seek are almost identical to those sought by the Western consumer, provided that these are Shariah-compliant.

It is this massive segment of the Muslim consumer market that multi-nationals (MNCs) are pursuing. This pursuit is being approached by MNCs in a most peculiar way; in their efforts to snatch a portion of the Islamic cake, MNCs are actually making Muslims more observant! They are creating *Halal* awareness among Muslims everywhere and, through their well-articulated marketing campaigns, forcing the *Halal* brand to be included on all sorts of products, even within Islamic markets which have historically never disputed the nature of the products available in their home markets and produced by their countrymen. It was always taken for granted that such products were *Halal*. These companies are vigorously driving *Halal* onto supermarket shelves, which in turn turns on their own production lines. In effect, MNCs are bringing Muslims closer to their God and in return Muslims are increasing the wealth of these companies' shareholders. It is a win–win situation for both parties; for multinationals the proliferation of *Halal* is big business, for Muslims consuming *Halal* is worship.

However, whether they both see it that way is another matter. If these companies could get this same message to Muslims, their chances of success among Muslims would increase greatly. Communicating this message effectively means that the existent historic, cultural and religious barriers separating MNCs and other aspiring firms from their target Muslim masses could be overcome through creating a religious-like image, a halo or positive image of these firms and reducing the tendency among Muslims to be suspicious of their operations. Although there is no guaranteed method of success in markets, Muslim or otherwise, the best strategy to use in Muslim markets is to support the aspirations of the Muslims' community leaders and followers to create better Muslims, i.e., more observant and benevolent.

Finally, selling products based on the *Halal* aspect alone will serve companies well in the short to medium run and as long as the number of competitors in that market remains relatively small. After that, *Halal* becomes only a core requirement or a qualifier but not a seller. Hopeful firms must link themselves more closely to the faith of the Muslim consumer in the long run if they wish to retain their precious and highly rewarding advantage in the attractive Islamic market.

The Non-Muslim Consumer

In order to understand who is a Muslim consumer one must first understand who is a non-Muslim consumer. Since no definitions have been provided in this regard before, at least not from a business or academic perspective, we tried in this book to present a definition that is both simple to understand, meaningful, culturally sensitive and thorough. After considering several alternatives and variables, it was decided that the definition that will be used throughout this book must include three different dimension; faith, brand and product. As a result, non-Muslim consumers have been defined as those who (a) adhere to faiths other than Islam, (b) buy products that are certified and labelled *Halal*, and/or (c) buy products that are known to be associated with Islamic countries.

(A) ADHERING TO FAITHS OTHER THAN ISLAM

This means three quarters of the world population or more than 4 billion consumers. The most likely non-Muslim consumers to patronize Islamic products are those who live in or near Muslim communities, or work or study with Muslim colleagues. For example, although the huge number of Muslims in India represent only a minority, most meat vendors in India today are Muslims and *Halal* is what they vend. Non-Muslim customers of *Halal* in India include the Indian Army, as well as many government institutions. Although the choice to buy *Halal* clearly suits the Muslim consumers serving in these institutions, it also makes business sense given the large number of *Halal* suppliers and the higher competition within the *Halal* market, which is driving prices downs and quality up.

(B) BUYING PRODUCTS THAT ARE CERTIFIED AND LABELLED *HALAL*

Halal brands, i.e., those showing a HALAL label, remain difficult to find outside Muslim ethnic shops and communities and their number is very limited when compared to the 100,000 kosher brands available on supermarkets' shelves everywhere.

However, there are many generic brands that are understood to be *Halal* without having the logo on them, e.g., the meat prepared at the local *Halal* slaughterhouses. Interested consumers know the nature of these products when purchasing from ethnic Islamic shops, which usually show the *Halal* logo as a sign or simple board indicating that the products sold there are *Halal*. These shops could be Arabic, Turkish, Persian, Pakistani, Indian, Bengali or African, etc.

The HALAL sign, logo, or label is usually written in both Arabic (حلال) and Roman scripts for several reasons.

1. *Avoid consumer alienation.* Since using one language in an ethnically diversified community might negatively affect consumer engagement, or might even be perceived to be culturally insensitive and thus lead to alienation of some consumers, Islamic businesses use both Arabic and Roman scripts as a way to appeal to all consumers within their trading area. Although some non-Muslims might recognize the Arabic logo, nearly all Muslims have at least a basic understanding and recognition of Arabic script since the Quran is recited only in the Arabic language and all Islamic prayers and rituals have to be performed in Arabic according to the teachings of Islam.

2. *Credibility.* The Arabic script will add authenticity and credibility to the business among its Muslim clientele since Arabic, as indicated above, is widely understood and religiously acknowledged by Muslims, both Arab and non-Arab.

3.   *Exoticness and ethnic.* The Arabic script is noticeably different than the Roman script, which adds a touch of exoticness to the business, as well as signalling that the products are also ethnic.

4.   *Visual recognition.* The Arabic script will help a business achieve better visual recognition, especially if the neighbouring businesses do not display the *Halal* sign.

(C) BUYING PRODUCTS THAT ARE KNOWN TO BE ASSOCIATED WITH ISLAMIC COUNTRIES PROVIDED THAT THEY ARE SHARIAH-COMPLIANT

It is taken for granted that products such as hummus, dates, couscous, falafel, etc. which originate from Islamic countries are generally *Halal.* However, a caution should be noted here in relation to the new Islamic states in Europe that are just discovering their Islamic identities. These newly Islamized countries have been under communist rule for such a long time that their citizens have forgotten many of the basic concepts of Islam. Although those citizens are keen to relearn about their religion they still have sometime before they can transform and incorporate their religious knowledge into business practices.

Motives Underlying Muslim Consumer's Decisions[1]

There are three factors driving the economic behaviour of Muslims: belief in the Day of Judgement and the hereafter, success and riches.

1.   Believing in the Day of Judgement and the life hereafter extends the time horizon of Muslims beyond death and closely interrelates life before and after death. This creates two effects as far as consumers' behaviour is concerned. First, the outcome of a choice of action is composed of its immediate effect in this life and its later effect in the life to come. Therefore, the utility derived from such a choice is the total of the present value of these two effects. Second, the number of alternative uses of one's income is increased by the inclusion of all the benefits that would be gained only in the hereafter. Examples of

---

1   This part of the book is adapted from Monzer Kahf's chapter: 'A contribution to the theory of consumer behavior in an Islamic society.' In *Studies in Islamic Economics* ed. Khurshid Ahmad (Jeddah, Saudi Arabia: International Center for Research in Islamic Economics, King Abdul Aziz University, and Markfield, UK: Islamic Foundation, 1979).

such alternative uses are interest-free lending, charity, securing of animal welfare and the welfare of future generations, improvement of communal life even when this has no immediate benefit for the individual, promotion and perpetuation of goodness, etc. These uses of income are excluded from Max Weber's theory of rationality unless they have some immediate utility. Thus many alternative uses of one's income may have positive utility in the Islamic culture; whereas their utility benefits in the capitalist rationalization may be zero.

2.   Success is defined in Islam in terms of the 'consent of Allah' and not in those of the accumulation of wealth. Virtue, righteousness and the fulfilment of the servanthood to Allah are key to His consent. Virtue and righteousness can be achieved through good actions and purification of human behaviour from evil and vice. Service and obedience to Allah may be rendered by the positive use of human capabilities and resources, given by Allah. This includes the full use and exploitation of everything given to mankind by Allah. According to the teachings of Islam, if a man really wants to serve Allah, the utilization of the natural and human resources made available to him is not only a privilege but also a duty and obligation prescribed by Allah. Therefore, material progress and perfection are in themselves moral values in Islam. Abstention and withdrawal from enjoyment and satisfaction from material life is in direct opposition to Islamic doctrines. Efficiency and the value of time are concepts made alive in human consciousness by the religion of Islam. After all, Islam urges and requires people to spend part of their time energy for the remembrance of Allah, the improvement of spiritual and moral surroundings, the propagation of virtue and goodness, etc. All this can only be done if part of human resources can be spared and liberated from the pursuit of consumption.

3.   The concept of wealth and income (Arabic: *Mal*) is unique in Islam. *Mal*, whether looked at as wealth or income, is a bounty from Allah; it is not an evil. Heaven is not only open to the poor, it is also and equally open to the rich. *Mal* is not a tool that may be used for good or evil. Poverty is, in some instances, associated with disbelief and riches are considered a gift from Allah. Since riches are a bounty from Him, they must be used for the benefit and satisfaction of

human wants. This is an implication of humble service to Allah. The Prophet said, 'Verily, Allah likes to see the trace of His bounty on His servant'.

4.   Finally, since *Mal* is a tool to buy goods and services which bring about satisfaction, it should be spent for that purpose and not hoarded. The concept of real income appears in another saying where real income is defined as the total of what is used for the purchase of goods and services that produce immediate satisfaction in this life plus that which is given away for causes that enrich one's life after.

In the light of these three principles, consumer behaviour in Islam can be described as a maximization of success (Arabic: *Falah*). Success may be defined, in the narrow sense, corresponding with consumer choice, as the level of obedience to Allah derived from the satisfaction of one's material wants and the exhibition of the effect of Allah's bounty by extracting enjoyment of the *Mal* given by Allah, and the enrichment of one's life after. The maximization of the consumer's success is subject to an income constraint determined by the level of spendable income. The latter is defined as total income minus planned change in wealth.

The exhibition of the trace of Allah's bounty affects the consumer's behaviour by raising the proportion of final spending to income because it implies an increase in spending on material wants and/or enrichment of one's life in the hereafter at each level of income. Consequently, at each level of income, final spending in the Muslim household is expected to be higher than in the non-Muslim family.

Serving the Modern Muslim Consumer

Businesses, allured by the grand potential of the Islamic market, are studying how to serve the modern Muslim consumer who is attracted to the glamorous Western lifestyles, yet observes the teachings of his/her religion. These consumers are looking for companies that will provide products and services that could help them lead their own glamorous Shariah-compliant lifestyle, they want brands that speak to them (Power and Abdullah 2009).

Muslim consumers in general are following their Western counterparts. Those consumers are well aware of this fact; it is deeply rooted in their psyche since the Prophet of Islam told them: 'You shall follow the paths of those who came before you, even if they entered a ruined hole of a desert monitor (Agama) you shall enter it behind them. The companions of the Prophet asked: [you mean] the Jews and the Christian? He said: who else?' Admiring the Western lifestyle is seen by Muslims as a prophecy. Such a prophecy is being translated into business opportunities by leading multinationals that seek to provide Islamic versions of mainstream Western products and services such as fast food, gyms and luxury hotels, to mention only a few. These businesses are allowing Muslims to express their religious principles through helping them buying Islamic; connecting to their Islamic roots by what they eat, wear and play. For example, traditional foods consumed by Muslims are now competing with pizzas, burgers and doughnuts in addition to an array of foods that have only recently entered the Muslim menu. KFC, Pizza Hut, Dominos, Dunkin Donuts and Subway chains have hundreds of *Halal* franchises across most Muslim countries. Moreover, Muslim travellers want luxurious hotels whose clients do not behave and dress provocatively, places where they can go to with their families (Power and Abdullah 2009). These and other demands from Muslim consumers are a sign of the new Islamic consumption identity, a market based on religious-compliant personal lifestyles.

The Behavior of Muslim Consumers

In this section specific dimensions describing the various aspects of the Muslim consumers' consumption patterns will be discussed and analyzed from the perspective of the religion of Islam, which, as explained earlier, plays a considerable role in the consumption decisions of Muslim consumers, from financing a car or arranging a house mortgage to having a light afternoon snack. Although to Muslims the rules concerning what, how and when to consume are part of their daily life, at first sight a non-Muslim might see them as numerous restrictions limiting one's choices of consumption. A careful look at them, however, will reveal that they are not restrictions but rules of consumption designed to organize Muslims' lives and enable them to strike a balance between the rational satisfaction of their endless desires and their limited needs. These rules help Muslims recognize that they are human with higher purposes in life rather than just consumers whose existence is justified only if they consume. They can be resembled to guideposts that draw the line between enough and indulgence.

Living these rules since birth, at home and in the community, makes living outside them clearly difficult. In fact, in the same way non-Muslims wonder how a Muslim could live with all of these 'restrictions' pertaining to everything they do, Muslims wonder how could others live without them. An Irish friend of mine told me during my PhD years in Dublin about a discussion he had with a Muslim student from the Arabian Peninsula about a steak. The Muslim student was convinced that *Haram* steaks smell bad when they are being cooked and validated his argument with the common belief among Muslims that animals not slaughtered the *Halal* way will retain much of their blood, which is burned during cooking thus producing a foul odour. My Irish friend, in turn, said the steaks smell lovely and she could not find anything bad about them. Both were convinced of their rightness on the issue. However, since there are no restrictions on food consumption in Catholicism, unlike in Islam, they had to go to a *Halal* restaurant because a Catholic may eat a *Halal* steak but a Muslim may not eat a steak that is not prepared according to the Islamic dietary laws.

What to Consume

The general rule in Islam is that *Halal* is the norm and *Haram* is the exception. However, since more focus is placed on *Haram*, even by Muslims, it is easily forgotten that *Haram* represents only a negligible fraction of God's overall creation. According to Islam, *Haram* is insignificant in the universe. In fact it could be likened to the forbidden tree in Paradise. While Adam and Eve could enjoy the infinite bounties of Paradise, they were forbidden to eat from one particular tree; only one tree in Paradise was *Haram* and all the other trees and fruits were *Halal*.

Having such a view of *Halal* and *Haram* will limit a company's abilities to innovate in the Islamic market because a company will have very limited room to manoeuvre at the very tight tip of the iceberg of Islamic consumption. The tip of that iceberg includes the three widely known Islamic prohibitions, i.e., prohibition of swine and their related products, prohibition of wine and its related products and prohibition of interest rates and its related products. A company producing or selling goods which may be affected by these prohibitions will need to be wary of everything it does, including its process, its ingredients and its selling practices. Since there are many restrictions a company is always at risk of violating some of them and thus falling victim to the massive propaganda machine of the Muslim consumer groups run by emotional, internet-savvy, young Muslims who don't necessarily hold a positive attitude towards Western products and producers.

The real opportunity for companies is to operate in the unseen part of that iceberg, the area of paradise where the infinite bounties are hardly seen by competitors, who remain fighting over the one forbidden tree, or the tight tip. Natural farming, technology and education, e.g., are much less regulated in Islam and it is much easier for a company to position its products as Islamic as there is much less risk of violating the Islamic guidelines such as those that exist in the dietary section of the Islamic laws. For example, a mobile phone company could add special features to its mobiles to appeal to Muslim consumers. Such additions might include prayer times, the direction of Mecca, an Islamic locator, the Islamic calendar and date, Quran recitations, Islamic songs, Islamic media and entertainment, etc. Moreover, a farmer raising cows in the green fields in the Netherlands is at little risk of violating Islamic guidelines since both the cow and the field are natural and don't fall within the three forbidden categories.

To summarize, the consumption of *Halal* is something that Muslims will be rewarded for as long as this consumption is in moderation. The Islamic rule in this regard is very clear: if a person starves himself needlessly then he is committing a bad deed and thus unless Allah forgives him his deed is punishable. Therefore, if a person eats well and maintains his body fit his action will be seen as a good deed that is worthy of reward by Allah. The same goes for the other numerous parts of our lives including entertainment, sports, sex, etc.

Finally, it is important to remember that *Halal* is the norm, not the exception, i.e., everything is *Halal* unless proven it is *Haram*. This is clearly stated by the Prophet: 'Eat what you feel like and wear what you feel like. But avoid two things: extravagance and arrogance.' A beautiful perfumed woman who liked clothes and making herself beautiful for her husband was seen one day by the Prophet's wife in bad shape so she asked her why she had changed. The woman said that her husband was among some of the companions of the Prophet who dedicated themselves to worship and abstained from women and eating meat, fasted the day and stayed awake during the night to worship, and she did not want to tempt her husband and make him forgo what he dedicated himself to. The wife of the Prophet told him of what some of his companions were doing. He went to them and told them that they should not be doing that and that they should eat meat, have intercourse with women, fast and break fast, pray and sleep, for that is what he was ordered by Allah.

How Much to Consume

A Muslim's proper consumption can best be characterized as moderation in the quantity acquired and consumed of that which is deemed *Halal*. As opposed to the prevailing attitude which expects consumption to be maximized, Islam greatly encourages moderate consumption; a Muslim consumer should only take what is enough and avoid needless consumption. The following Islamic teachings clearly set forth the guidelines for the Muslim consumers' proper consumption.

FOOD CONSUMPTION

Allah says in the Quran:

> *Say (O Muhammad): Who has forbidden the adornment with clothes given by Allâh, which He has produced for His slaves, and At-Taiyyibât [all kinds of Halâl (lawful) things] of food? Say: They are, in the life of this world, for those who believe, (and) exclusively for them (believers) on the Day of Resurrection (the disbelievers will not share them). Thus We explain the Ayât (Islâmic laws) in detail for people who have knowledge ...*
>
> *Quran 7:31*

These divine words clearly tell believers that they must not abstain from that which Allah has given to them, i.e., enjoying food and drink. This enjoyment, however, must be within limits that help the Muslim avoid indulgence yet gain the benefits. These limits are clarified in the teachings of the Prophet Mohammad where He says: 'A believer eats in one intestine (is satisfied with a little food), and a kafir (unbeliever) eats in seven intestines (eats much food)', and 'A human has not filled a container worse than his belly. The son of Adam should be content with few bites that maintain his strength. But if he must do that [eating more than a few bites because he cannot control his cravings] then one third [of his stomach] is for his food, one third for his drink, and one third for his breath.' Words that could easily be attributed to a dietician!

CLOTHES CONSUMPTION

Allah says in the Quran: 'O Children of Adam! Take your adornment while praying and going round the Ka'bah …' (Quran 7:31), and 'Say (O Muhammad): Who has forbidden the adornment with clothes given by Allah, which He has produced for His slaves …' (Quran 7:32). In these two verses from the seventh chapter in the Quran Allah asks Muslims to wear good clothes and to beautify themselves, but again without extravagance. The difference between what is acceptable and extravagance is explained in the teachings of the Prophet:

1.   'Gold and silk are forbidden for the males of my nation and allowed for their females.'

2.   'Never let your lower garment go below the ankles because that is arrogance. And Allah does not like arrogance.'

To clarify further, a dress should (Khalid n.d.):

1.   Cover specific parts of the body adequately. For men, it is the middle part of the body from navel to knee. For women, it is the entire body except hands and face. These parts must never be exposed to any other person (except in case of genuine need, e.g., medical treatment). In addition, the cloth must be neither see-through nor tight fitting.

2.   Provide for decent appearance. For men, this extends the coverage requirements to include most of the body. For women, the essential requirement is that their dress should identify them as respectable ladies.

3.   The dress design must avoid three deadly sins: showing off, arrogance and self-indulgence.

Finally, it is important to note that Islam has not prescribed a particular dress style, giving Muslims ample room to accommodate their needs, circumstances and tastes. However, these principles are for everyone and for ever. Any garment that accommodates these principles will be Islamic dress (Khalid n.d.).

When to Consume

The Muslim consumer is not a non-stop consumption machine and is not set on an endless consumption spree, consuming as much as his body and time tolerate or, in the process of that consumption, stretching his finances thin and wide. A Muslim's consumption is guided by two main factors: the existence of a need, and/or the performance of a religious duty or ritual.

EXISTENCE OF A NEED

Using Maslow's hierarchy, humans' needs range between physical requirements that are necessary for an abstract survival to self actualization which comes after one has acquired many of the worldly things he or she wished for earlier. The insistence of these higher needs is not less than the lower needs of food, safety and companionship, and people tend to pursue them vigorously. Some Muslim scholars add a higher dimension to the hierarchy of needs and they call it the need to believe, or faith.

The various needs in this hierarchy are widely accepted among scholars and apply to people in different cultures, although with some distinction that allows for certain-specific sensitivities and peculiarities to be observed.

At the lower level of needs, and as far as the basic need for food is concerned Islam clearly describes when and how much to eat: 'We are a nation [Muslims] that don't eat until we become hungry, and if we eat, we don't eat our fill (Prophet Mohammad).' This teaching has been deeply integrated into the dining manners of Arab Muslims, especially at banquet invitations from family, friends and others. Filling one's plate at these occasions will raise many eyebrows and elicit many quiet yet unfavourable comments. Going for a second round is even worse, unless one is going to get sweets or drinks. To help reduce the amount of food consumed a Muslim is encouraged to converse when dining. Longer conversations will allow the body to absorb nutrients from the food and thus reduce cravings and helps a diner feel full with a lesser amount of food.

At the highest level of needs, faith, adherents are also required to practise it in moderation in order to avoid extreme practices that could actually have negative outcomes. An adherent to Islam could theoretically fast any number of days in addition to the Muslim fasting month of Ramadan, could volunteer to pray all night long for as many nights he or she wished, and could spend his or her entire fortune in charity. However, doing any of these to the extreme is greatly discouraged by Islam. The Prophet teaches 'This religion is made easy, yet whoever contests with it will be defeated.' This means that Muslims should 'take it easy' when practising their faith; Allah knows our limits and tolerances and trying to bypass these will not bring us closer to Him or make Him more satisfied with our unwarranted extra deeds. It is good that a Muslim wakes up at night and prays for sometime but it is wrong that he stays awake the whole night praying because that will prevent him from attending to his worldly affairs. Fasting for many months in the year will weaken him. Spending all of his fortune on charities will send him and his family into poverty. Abstinence from natural desires is not the way of Islam. The Prophet teaches: 'But I pray and sleep, I fast and I breakfast, I eat meat, and I marry women and those who do not follow my Sunnah [way] are not of me', 'The best fasting is that of Allah's Apostle David, he used to fast a day and break fast a day' and:

> In the year of the last Hajj of the Prophet I became seriously ill and the Prophet used to visit me inquiring about my health. I told him, I am reduced to this state because of illness and I am wealthy and have no inheritors except a daughter. Should I give all of my property in charity? He said, no. I asked, half? He said, no. Then I asked, one-third? The Prophet said a third and a third is too much; you would better leave your inheritors wealthy rather than leaving them poor, begging others. You will be rewarded for whatever you spend for Allah's sake even if it were a morsel which you put in your wife's mouth.

Giving in charity is a highly praised deed in Islam, as long as it is within reason.

How to Consume

Islam places special emphasis on the social aspect of life. It encourages people to interact and to mix together. It also encourages collective actions and cooperation between adherents who are encouraged to know one another. Many of the pure acts of worship in Islam are designed to instil a community spirit, like Friday and Eid Prayers (end of Ramadan and end of hajj) that must be performed in congregation (Badawi 2007). Praying in congregation strengthens the ties between people by giving them the opportunity to interact with each other and discuss their issues in a holy place. Similarly, fasting has many social aspects: it causes Muslims to feel the starvation and the agony of the poor and deprived in society and encourages them to extend their hands in help towards them. The hajj undoubtedly is the largest religious and social convention, bringing millions of people from around the globe into one arena to strengthen their ties, develop their skills and exchange ideas and opinions as to how to improve their situations. Charity also plays an important social role in Islam by causing Muslims to think that they themselves are responsible for bridging the gap between the rich and the poor as well as for sharing their own wealth with the needy (revertmuslims.com 2009).

Moreover, although it is clear in Islam that dining alone is perfectly acceptable, it is encouraged that people dine in groups for the sake of blessing. 'The Companions of the Prophet said: Apostle of Allah we eat but we are not satisfied. He said: Perhaps you eat separately. They replied: Yes. He said: If you gather together at your food and mention Allah's name, you will be blessed in it.' To summarize, Islam greatly encourages group activities; the Prophet says 'Allah's extends his hand in help to the group.'

The Muslim Consumer Demographics

A comprehensive demographic study of more than 232 countries conducted by the Pew Research Center in October 2009 mapped the demographics of the Muslim population and found that there are 1.57 billion Muslims around the world and on all continents, accounting for almost one in four people. Most Muslims are Sunni (87–90 per cent) following the Quran and the Sunnah, i.e., life of the Prophet Mohammad, while the vast majority of the remainder (10–13 per cent) are Shi'a. According to the study more than 60 per cent of the Muslim population is in Asia and about 20 per cent is in the Middle East and North Africa. The Middle East and North Africa region – mostly Arab Muslims – has the highest percentage of Muslim-majority countries. But more than 300 million Muslims, or one-fifth of the Muslim population, live in countries where Muslims are a minority group, often quite a large group. India, e.g., has the third-largest population of Muslims worldwide with 161 million Muslims (Lugo 2009). Of the 232 countries and territories included in the Pew Research Center study, 50 are Muslim-majority.

Although it is hard to say that all of these populations are homogeneous, if only due to the sheer number alone, it is still possible to draw some common characteristics that are shared between most of them due to the nature of the religion of Islam, the mostly shared history and the relatively similar present circumstances, ambitions and challenges. These characteristics include:

1.   Muslims have large families.

2.   Muslims live in and support extended families where successive generations take care of each other. It is very common to find three generations living in the same house.

3.   The Muslim family is structured around creating a prosperous environment for the family's children and women. This is the religious duty of every Muslim.

4.   Muslim populations are young: the majority of Muslims are less than 30 years old.

5.   Contrary to common stereotypes, Muslim women play a central role in the family with most family-related decisions being made directly or indirectly by them. Many of them also engage in entrepreneurial activities, often home-based, to support families.

6.   Older people are well regarded and respected. Elders have a lot of say in most family decisions especially in extended families.

7.   All Muslims – that's more than one and a half billion – are required to perform hajj once in a lifetime. Hajj is a religious journey to Mecca. Hajj and Umrah (smaller hajj) generated nearly $30 billion for Saudi Arabia in 2009 from organizing pilgrimages to Islamic holy places. The figure covers travelling, accommodation and living expenses, as well as cost of animals for sacrifices (Ali 2009). The 1.57 billion would-be pilgrims could generate as much as $16 trillion worth of economic activity.

8.   Muslims are usually more likely to be practising than are adherents of other major world religions. This, in turn, stimulates massive economic activities centred around the various religious rituals such as hajj, fasting during the month of Ramadan, supporting charities, praying and offering sacrifices, in addition to those around rituals pertaining to the worldly lives of Muslims such as marriages, visitations, congregations and others.

9.   Muslims admire Western lifestyles but they cannot embrace them because many of them are seen as being contradictory to the Islamic laws. The West is the ultimate destination for Muslim students, the preferred holiday destination for wealthy Muslims and the symbol of quality and honesty for Muslim businessmen, while Western medical institutions are the last refuge for Muslims with difficult illnesses.

10.   Even when some Muslims are not particularly observant they tend to trust people who are considered religious. Religious people are the real community leaders among Muslims and they command a great deal of power and authority. They are well organized, well connected and publicity experts. Their influence shouldn't be ignored by any aspirant firm.

Country-specific and Culture-specific Attitudes of the Muslim Consumer

Muslim consumers are very sensitive to certain consumption patterns and may restrict their consumption or refrain from purchasing products or brands that are perceived to be associated with specific countries believed to be hostile to Muslims, which is contrary to the common belief that Muslim consumers are generally anti-Western. Muslims have high regard for German products, e.g., despite Germany being a Western country. This points to a very important fact that is usually overlooked when discussing Muslim consumers and that fact is Muslims attitudes are usually country-specific not culture-specific. Muslims don't loathe the West as is commonly stereotyped in literature and media. The question that is often asked in some media outlets – 'Why do they [the Muslims] hate us [the West]' – has no answer, simply because they don't. This distinctive attitude by Muslims is actually a core religious teaching stated clearly in the Quran; one is not to be held accountable for another's actions. 'Say: Shall I seek a lord other than Allâh, while He is the Lord of all things? No person earns any (sin) except against himself (only), and no bearer of burdens shall bear the burden of another. Then unto your Lord is your return, so He will tell you that wherein you have been differing' (Quran 6:164).

The clear, and religious, distinction in the minds and hearts of the Muslim consumers between country-specific and culture-specific attitudes has significant implications for the Western companies engaged in or considering engaging the Muslim market. While Danish products have been largely shunned by the Muslim consumers, as a result of the fallout of the cartoons that were published in Danish media depicting Mohammad, the Prophet of Islam, in a less than respectable way, the products of neighbouring Germany continue to enjoy a highly regarded position in the Muslim markets. Moreover, while Danish exports to the Islamic world have dwindled, those of the nearby Netherlands have escaped relatively unharmed.

Such a distinction creates an opportunity for these companies. Being associated with a country that is positively perceived by Muslims will result in increased demand for its products. A company that is welcomed by the Muslim consumer means that it is not seen as anti-Islamic, unlike companies associated with countries that are perceived negatively, which will be almost automatically be seen as anti-Islamic. The attitude of the Muslim consumer, whether positive or negative, is always linked to religion and/or justified by religion. Thus consuming products originating from certain countries becomes a sin and from others a good deed. Indeed a very tricky situation that companies find tricky to manoeuvre. However, there are several ways to avoid a negative image.

Disassociation from 'Hostile' Countries

Since religion plays a central role in the Muslim consumer decision-making process, all things, including countries, products and individuals, can be classified into one of three categories: bad, good or neutral. A 'hostile' country is one which is involved or has been involved recently in actions that are perceived to be contradictory to the beliefs of Muslim consumers, while a 'good' country is that doing the opposite. The image of the country will be involuntarily projected on the companies associated with it. Thus, companies need to carefully choose with whom they should be associated if they plan to deal with Muslim consumers.

Neutral classification brands are those that are classified by Muslim consumers as neither good nor bad. Company in this category can build whatever image it desires for itself and its brands. However, it is important to note here that many multinationals merely copy their image into the Muslim market with only minor cosmetic changes and facelifts. A classical example is that of a famous drug company marketing a new remedy in the United Arab Emirates which tried to avoid possible mistakes in language by using pictures instead of words. The first picture on the left was of someone ill, the next picture showed the person taking the medication, the final picture on the right showed a healthy person. What Arab consumers saw was a healthy person taking the remedy and then falling ill; the company failed to notice that Arabs read from right to left.

On the other hand, a company can get away with many wrongdoings and slip unharmed in the Muslim market as long as it doesn't do something that scratches, even remotely, the religion of Islam. Religion to Muslim consumers is highly regarded even by those who are not easily classified as religious people. When Nike introduced a new design of sports shoe with a symbol on them which looked like the Arabic script for 'God', a massive campaign ensued in which masses of Muslim consumers participated forcing the company to apologize and withdraw the design from the market. It is worth noting here that Nike in the Arab world used to be associated with Westernized lifestyles mainly adopted by people who are not classified as religious.

To disassociate a company from a country that is at risk of confrontation – political or otherwise – with Muslim countries, organizations or groups, an MNC should be truly a multinational, i.e., belong to the world as a whole not to specific country or a few elite ones. It should have international citizenship so that consumers all over the world can say that this MNC is theirs. Having an international citizenship will make the company immune to the immense political changes associated with the Middle East, and consequently with the wider Muslim population.

Association with 'Friendly' Countries

Another approach to enhance the company's image in the Muslim consumers' minds is to be actually associated with countries that are perceived positively, or at least neutral. Switzerland, despite all of the chronic hostilities between Muslims and some Western powers historically and in the present, remains a favourite destination for Arab oil money. Swiss products in the Middle East have an almost sanctified status, up to this point at least, since the vote to ban the construction of minarets in mosques in November 2009 will have a negative long-term effect on the country's image. This approach is nonetheless risky. Due to the political turmoil the world has plunged into and with new coalitions emerging, a friend today could be a foe tomorrow. Strongly associating a company's image with a specific country could have catastrophic consequences. The massive boycott of the Danish products came almost out of the blue: Danish producers didn't anticipate it and Muslim consumers never had any previous concerns about Denmark because that country was relatively unknown to them. As such its products enjoyed a market relatively void of serious international competition; its brands easily pushed their way into refrigerators in Muslim homes. It is very difficult to find a Muslim who doesn't know what Puck is. Danish brands, had they been positioned since the start as international instead of Danish, would have suffered much less from the boycott.

Image Management

To manage the company's or country's image successfully the political concerns of Muslim consumers must be addressed. The UK, which is much better at image management than the USA, enjoys a prominent position in the Middle Eastern market despite being a major partner to the US in all hostilities with Muslims. There are more Range Rovers in the United Arab Emirates than in the whole of Europe, aside from the UK itself. France, which also does a relatively good job with image management (although not as good as the UK), enjoys a superior position in the bottled water market; French water is sold at very high premiums when compared to local and regional brands. Spanish olive products crowd the shelves of Arab supermarkets and Danish dairy products were an Arab favourite before Denmark's fall from approval.

Image management should be pursued as a remedy if and when a company's or a country's image is distorted for some reason, usually political or religious. To endeavour to build a reputation at any price – maybe provoking target market – and then to try and manage that reputation is not a wise choice when consumers as emotional as the Muslim consumers are concerned. Unfortunately, consumers are unforgiving and to them 'once a sinner is always a sinner', rarely would they heed to the teachings of their religion which greatly praises the attribute of being able to forgive. Thus, the notions of 'any publicity is good publicity' or 'I don't care what they say about me as long as they spell my name right' is an approach that should be avoided in most cases, such as in cross-cultural marketing where religion might be involved.

Conclusion

The influence of the religion of Islam on the behaviour of its followers cannot be overestimated. The Islamic law, the Shariah, is so comprehensive that it describes what a Muslim should and should not do during his/her entire waking hours. The Muslim begins his day at dawn with ablutions and performing the dawn prayers and ends it with night prayer nearly two hours after sunset. Three other prayers have to be performed between dawn and night at specified times and each is usually done with a separate ablution. Being in contact with the Quran and the Sunnah five times a day will undoubtedly have a profound effect on a Muslim's behaviour. Add to that having to fast an entire month each year, giving two obligatory alms (the 2.5 per cent money tax and the breakfast tax at the end of Ramadan), giving voluntary donations according to one's means, performing hajj and attending Friday prayers, end of Ramadan prayers and end of hajj prayers. A Muslim's life revolves around the script and what it instructs. Abiding by it is a worship that will bring a Muslim closer to Allah. A Muslim's decisions are made with one clear aim in mind and that is to please Allah, the creator, the merciful and the companionate. As a result, any decision or course of action that will upset Allah will not be considered.

Although one might argue that not all Muslims are God-fearing and thus the above discussion doesn't apply to them, the influence of observant Muslims and overly Islamic cultural norms and traditions are so immense in Islamic society that it becomes difficult for the less observant Muslims not to be observant, at least in public.

International marketers cannot afford to ignore the religious factor in the decision making process of the Muslim consumer. Regardless of the background of the marketer, be it capitalism, liberalism, socialism or something else, those consumers have a different orientation towards life that might not exactly fit with the pre-packaged marketing formulas or with the prevalent marketing wisdom. They have a unique code of practice and they embrace that code with zeal. Non-conforming marketers will find themselves on a collision course with their prospects and customers and their brands will soon be removed from the shelves of supermarkets in Muslim countries.

International marketers must help Muslims become more observant and must include that fact in their marketing communications. I was once in Mecca amid a sea of pilgrims from all over the world. The ones sitting beside me were, as far as could tell, from Indonesia or Malaysia. I was silently praising God for all the bounties he had bestowed upon me. While I was doing that I kept hearing the sound of successive clicks the source of which which I couldn't immediately identify. After a little concentration I saw that my Asia-Pacific brothers were praising God with the help of technology; they were using little hand-held devices, very simple, to count and record how many times they praised! I don't know what brand was carved on the Praiser, but the manufacturing firm has made it all the way to Mecca.

Key terms:

- The Muslim consumer
- Shariah-compliant Muslims
- The non-Muslim consumer
- *Halal* logos
- Muslim consumer behaviour
- Muslim consumer demographics
- 'Hostile' and friendly countries of origin.

References

Ali, J. (2009). 'Haj vital to Saudi economy.' *Gulf News*. 29 November.

Badawi, J. (2007). 'Social relationships in Islam.' Retrieved 1 December, 2009, from http://www.readingislam.com/servlet/Satellite?c=Article_C&cid=1173 695223318&pagename=Zone-English-Discover_Islam%2FDIELayout.

Khalid, B. (n.d.). 'The Islamic dress code.' Retrieved 28 November 2009 from http://www.albalagh.net/food_for_thought/dress.shtml.

Lugo, L. (2009). 'Mapping the global Muslim population: a report on the size and distribution of the world's Muslim population.' Pew Research Center. Retrieved 1 December 2009 from http://pewforum.org/uploadedfiles/Topics/Demographics/Muslimpopulation.pdf.

Power, C. and S. Abdullah (2009). 'Buying Muslim.' *Time South Pacific* (Australia/New Zealand edition) 173(20): 31–4.

revertmuslims.com. (2009). 'Social life in Islam.' Retrieved 1 December, 2009, from http://www.revertmuslims.com/islam/social_life_in_islam.htm.

8

Islamic Branding: Concepts and Background[1]

There is a new big thing in the world of marketing and it is green, not the familiar grass-green of the environment, but a deeper green – the traditional color of Islam.

Young 2007

Learning Objectives

After reading this chapter, you should be able to:

- Compare religious and ethnic branding with Islamic branding
- Differentiate between Halal and kosher as religious products
- Differentiate between Islamic products and Islamic brands
- Identify the various types of Islamic branding
- Identify the Halal customers
- Identify the Halal categories
- Describe the importance of innovation in Halal
- Describe the difficulties in Halal certification
- Describe the growing importance of Halal logistics.

---

1   This chapter has been previously published as Alserhan, B. A. (2010). 'Islamic branding: A conceptualization of related terms.' *Journal of Brand Management* 18: 34–49.

Introduction

Religious brands like *Halal* and kosher can capture a craving for purity that goes beyond the religious duty of their faithful adherents. The vast majority of kosher customers are not of the Jewish faith and, likewise, many Shariah-compliant firms reveal that not all of their customers are Muslims. For example, at the Jawhara Hotels, an alcohol-free Arabian Gulf chain, 60 per cent of the clientele are non-Muslims, drawn by the hotels' serenity and family-friendly atmosphere. Likewise, a quarter of the Dutch-based cookie and chocolate company Marhaba's customers are non-Muslims (Power and Abdullah 2009). While Muslims consume 16 per cent of kosher products in the US alone, demand for *Halal* food products by Jewish and Christian consumers is increasing as those customers become aware of the *Halal* brand. These religious products, unlike ethnic products which base their appeal mainly on being exotic, are associated with the more profound concepts of cleanliness, purity and kindness, in addition to being different and exotic.

Islamic religious brands, or *Halal* brands, are prepared according to the Islamic principles that guide what is permitted not just in the food industry but also in cosmetics, pharmaceuticals, logistics, clothing, finance, hospitality and banking (Minkus-McKenna 2007), thus extending the religious umbrella much more widely than kosher or ethnic products, which are mainly associated with the food industry. Although this extension provides a much greater opportunity for a diverse mass of businesses to engage profitably, the *Halal* market remained unexplored by the majority of non-Muslim multinational corporations until very recently and the relatively small number of MNCs that dared to engage *Halal* at an earlier stage now enjoy the results of their timely intervention; they dominate 90 per cent of the *Halal* food market.

Non-Muslim MNCs like Nestlé, Unilever, L'Oréal, Colgate, Baskin Robbins and Campbell Soup, among others, continue to invest heavily in addressing the Islamic dietary, lifestyle and consumption requirements. For example, at the Nestlé corner at the third annual World Halal Forum WHF exhibition, information on Shariah-compliant Smarties, PowerBars, Maggi Noodles, ice cream and Koko Krunch breakfast cereal was displayed. Moreover, Nestlé is investing CHF 85 million in Malaysia in 2009 to meet the increasing demand for *Halal* products of which Nestlé Malaysia is the Centre of Excellence. The investment supports the setting up of new regional plants for Nescafé and non-dairy creamer as well as the expansion of its Maggi facilities (Power 2008). These companies build on and transform the image of their brands from being international to being Islamic, i.e., accepted by the Muslim consumer as *Halal* brands. A successful transformation can be immensely beneficial to jump start an MNC's brand in an Islamic market. International corporate brands are only significant if they successfully translate the core value proposition of the corporate offering into the new Islamic market, a difficult task that can be achieved only when the entire firm lives and breathes the brand and every aspect of the firm reflects the brand values and essence (Melewar and Walker 2003), i.e., *Halal*.

This chapter aims to provide a better understanding of Islamic branding through conceptualizing the terms relevant to firms' brand Islamization efforts. It emphasizes the importance of Muslims as a distinct potential market that remains noticeably under-researched and demonstrates that the novelty of the topic itself is worthy of consideration since research about Islamic branding is non-existent despite the huge potential the Islamic market presents; it also defines and differentiates between the concepts of Islamic products and Islamic brands, conceptualizes the major branding considerations an Islamizing firm needs to consider and provides a valuable source of insights for future research as well as a benchmark for practitioners.

Importance of Islamic Branding

In order to engage the *Halal* market, firms need to employ brand Islamization strategies based on information obtained from the Islamic market, including customers, competitors and the business environment. With such information, firms can further develop their organizational values, norms, practices and structure in order to be appreciative of the novelty of the Islamic market.

Firms willing to target Muslim consumers need different strategies to those used for targeting traditional consumers. Their marketing strategies must be aligned with Islamic values, standards and guidelines. However, research has so far been characterized as being narrowly focused and limited to understanding marketing decisions based on Western ideologies and principles (Zakaria and Abdul-Talib forthcoming). According to Paul Tempral, an expert on Islamic branding: 'To date, there has been little formal research into the branding issues associated with serving these markets – which represent a sizeable commercial opportunity for many brand owners and developers' (Temporal 2008).

Islam creates an identifiable culture because it provides a way of life for people at both organizational and personal levels. The challenges in doing business in Islamic countries thus come from the fact that Muslims have a different set of values and beliefs that guide their behaviour in both business and non-business situations. The importance of these sets of values in business have only recently come to the attention of world marketers. Recognizing a substantial opportunity in this market, non-Muslim multinationals like Tesco, McDonald's and Nestlé, as well as many others, have massively expanded their Islamic operations; it is estimated that they control 90 per cent of the global *Halal* market. These and many other mainstream companies are making significant programs specifically designed for the Muslim consumer.

Understanding the Muslim consumer mandates that the strategic market-orientation of these firms be assessed and implemented differently since related decisions are culturally bound; different consumer segments require different approaches. Achieving marketing mix standardization when implementing a marketing strategy in an international market is difficult (Kustin 2004), and in fact it has been suggested that standardization is only effective in homogeneous markets (Jain 1989) while adaptation and localization strategies are needed in heterogeneous, i.e., Islamic or Western markets (Duncan and Ramaprasad 1995). Nestlé, in a statement posted in its website's FAQs, says:

> *Nestlé encourages its national operations to adapt products locally, in order to respect the local, regional and national habits and the tastes, cultural and religious backgrounds of consumers as well as their purchasing power. While all products must correspond to our quality requirements, they vary extensively in composition, recipe, packaging and branding.*

Religion as a Brand

According to William Drenttel in his emotional 'My Country is not a Brand':

> *Branding has its value in commerce and its leads to better commercial communication, to understanding the needs of an audience, or building long-term relationships with consumers. However, when the vocabulary of a nation's foreign policy is the vocabulary of branding, then it is, in fact, selling Uncle Ben's Rice. This transaction, with the vocabulary of the supermarket counter, is not how I envision my country speaking to*

the rest of the world. The symbol for a country should not be created by branding experts.

Drenttel 2004

Drenttel's comments might apply even more closely to major world religions such as Islam, Judaism and Christianity that are being vigorously commercialized. Nonetheless, regardless of what one might think about the commercialization of religions or national symbols, such a trend has become an acknowledged fact in the business world that needs to be contended with.

Having said that, it is worth noting that commercializing Islam is much less likely to occur due to the nature and teachings of the Islamic faith itself. In Islam there are clear and strict conditions that must be adhered to before a firm can get on the marketing vehicle of religion. In Islam brands cannot be Shariah-compliant until they fulfil many conditions related to ingredients, logistics, impacts and intentions. Such fulfilment results in *Halal* or wholesome products. In this regard religion plays an active role in transforming businesses into ethical entities whose goals rise above sales and revenues. Hence, it is my view that firms enduring the agony of changing their production processes and marketing practices to become Shariah-compliant have earned the right to use the words '*Halal* and Islamic' to support their marketing efforts. I don't see much harm in utilizing religion to improve the business environment or make life better in a more general sense. After all, isn't that what religion is supposed to do?

Nonetheless, some manufacturers have gone too far in their efforts to commercialize Islam. Mecca Cola is the perfect example. The company, building on negative Muslim sentiments, claimed to have introduced the Islamic alternative to Coca-Cola. As usual people who bought the drink disposed of the bottles and cans in the garbage while children used the bottles as an object to kick. Muslims didn't do anything and continued to purchase the drink. However, if such a product had been introduced by a non-Muslim company the fallout would have been extreme and the company might have been labelled as anti-Islamic for disgracing the name of their most holy place. As such, non-Muslim companies must be extra cautious; their white dress can easily spot.

Islamic Branding Defined

Islamic branding can be defined in three different ways, in all of which the descriptor 'Islamic' is used: Islamic brands by compliance (religion), by origin or by customer.

ISLAMIC BRANDS BY RELIGION

Islamic brands that base their appeal strictly on being Shariah-compliant are currently concentrated in the finance and food sectors and, to a lesser degree, in the growing sector of *Halal* logistics. These brands are intended to appeal specifically to the Muslim consumer. Increasingly however, many of these brands are broadening their appeal to attract other customers. For example, more than 60 per cent of the customers of Islamic hotels in Dubai are non-Muslims.

ISLAMIC BRANDS BY ORIGIN

These are brands that acquire the description 'Islamic' mainly because they originate from Islamic countries. Examples include airlines such as Emirates Airlines, telecoms such as the Emirati Etisalat and the Egyptian Orascom, and industry such as the Saudi SABIC. These companies don't promote themselves as Shariah-compliant since some of them are clearly non-compliant; the UAE Emirates and Etihad Airlines both serve alcohol to their customers, which clearly goes against the teachings of Islam. Telecoms also don't promote themselves Islamically since they are not religious in character; they apply the promotional methods of other multinational telecoms.

ISLAMIC BRANDS BY CUSTOMER

The third type of Islamic branding is that describing brands that emanate from non-Islamic countries yet are designed specially to target the Muslim consumer. Although these brands are usually owned by non-Muslims they are described as Islamic because of their target customers, i.e., Muslims. They include the *Halal* brands of multinationals such as Nestlé, Unilever, L'Oréal, McDonalds, KFC, and many others. These MNCs are investing heavily in cultivating the largely vacant Islamic markets. As a result of their efforts they now dominate 90 per cent of the Islamic food, cosmetics and health markets.

Islamic brands by customer are these that are owned by MNCs that have the skills and the know-how of branding, skills that so far eluded the Islamic companies operating under the slogan of 'we are Muslim', an approach that was taken for granted until they began facing fierce competition from non-Muslim companies utilizing a world-class branding expertise to excel in satisfying the specific needs of the observant Muslim consumer. Both Shariah-compliant brands provided by Muslim companies and Islamized brands provided by MNCs share an important theme: their main attraction is the concept of *Halal*, unlike the second category of brands that are classified as Islamic by origin and appeal to customers using the traditional, not the value-laden Islamic marketing approach.

Islamic Brands vs. Islamic Products

While it might be politically or geographically acceptable to describe all products originating from Islamic countries as Islamic, it would be religiously incorrect to do so in cases of Shariah non-compliant products since a non-compliant product cannot be branded as Islamic. Because brands are closely linked to emotions, even more so when religion is involved, such a distinction becomes necessary for companies planning to approach consumers in Islamic markets under a religious slogan.

In the case of the first two types of branding; Islamic brands by compliance and Islamic brands by country of origin, there is still some confusion as to the difference between Islamic brands and Islamic products since they are used in many cases interchangeably. It is not until the difference between these two is recognized and abridged that Islamic branding can fulfil its potential (Young 2007). For example, Turkey is a Muslim country yet its total wine production in 2005 was an enormous 287,000 hl according to the International Organization of Vine and Wine. Any business person with the slightest knowledge about Islam would know that wine is forbidden and strongly condemned in Islam; there is no such thing as Islamic or *Halal* wine. Even Barbican doesn't promote its non-alcoholic beer as beer in the Muslim market but rather as a malt drink seen by many in the Muslim world as good for the kidneys! Therefore, labouring to brand Turkish wine as an Islamic product wouldn't make much sense despite Turkey being 98 per cent Muslim in terms of population and despite being home of the Ottoman caliphate which led the Islamic world for many centuries. Another example would be the 350,000 pigs raised by Egyptian farmers (all pigs in Egypt were slaughtered in 2009 in the wake of Swine Flu). Islam takes such a strong stand against the consumption of pig products that the Egyptian pigs became associated in the Muslim psyche with a multitude of social and physical illnesses, in addition to being a major sin. The answer to the joke question of how to slaughter pigs in a *Halal* way to make them Islamic has much wider applications; a product which is *Haram* by nature cannot be made Islamic or *Halal* by process. Islam approves only wholesome products that have been raised, prepared and transported wholesomely from 'farm to table', and to the Muslim consumer, pigs and alcohol and their by-products are not wholesome in the first place.

MNCs need to learn to distinguish between these two in order to communicate more effectively with their potential Muslim markets.

Generally, engaging these markets has two requirements: providing Shariah-compliant products and relocating to Muslim markets. Fulfilling these requirements will not guarantee success but will significantly improve an MNC's chances of it. However, to relocate while not paying attention to the core requirement of being Shariah-compliant will get these companies nowhere in their efforts to brand themselves as Islamic. Although the location will support an MNC's efforts in that regard, it is only secondary to Shariah-compliance.

Relocating to Muslim Markets

Relocating to Muslim markets could be a significant differentiating factor since it provides assurance to the Muslim consumer in several ways. First, MNCs with national subsidiaries tend to employ mostly nationals. In the case of MNCs operating in Muslim countries, it is safe to say that most of their employees in these subsidiaries will be Muslims, which clearly sends the message that these products are produced by Muslims for Muslims who wouldn't be producing non-Shariah-compliant products. Another advantage is that the product logistics will be perceived as *Halal*, i.e., not contaminated during storage, shipping and, in some cases, not shipped through or by nations or companies that are being perceived negatively by the Muslim consumer. A third advantage would be an improved image if these MNCs sourced ingredients locally. Local suppliers who profit from their business relationships with the MNC will work as dedicated representatives within their Muslim communities. Sourcing input locally further strengthens the company's image as Shariah-compliant since it is taken for granted that all foodstuffs produced in Muslim countries are *Halal*.

Relocation may, however, bring a disadvantage: consumers in these markets may perceive the quality of locally produced items as lesser than those produced internationally. Some time must lapse before the local subsidiary can establish itself as a quality producer that stands on an equal footing with its mother company, with local staff who are competent and locally sourced material of comparable quality to material sourced internationally.

The Muslim markets in this book are defined as those comprised of people adhering to the Islamic faith. To them the word Islamic also has geo-political connotations but when it comes consumption, *Halal* becomes a basic qualifying condition and only then all other supplementations and enhancements become differentiating factors. A product that is not *Halal* yet intended for Islamic markets will mostly likely fail regardless of how it is packaged or offered. The elegant design and packaging of a bottle of Champaign will not lure Muslim consumers into buying it; the rule is *Halal* first then enhancements.

The *Halal* Market

'We are now at the point where Halal is more than a religious duty. Halal is big business: counting Islamic finance, as well as drugs and foodstuffs, and is dovetailing with contemporary consumer concerns from animal welfare to GM crops and fair trade' (Power 2008). An MNC tapping into the vast *Halal* market makes it more global in terms of attending to the needs of Muslims as a new segment of customers; companies are not going to be truly global unless they serve this market (Power and Gatsiounis 2007). For example, Nestlé engaged with the *Halal* industry very early in comparison to other manufacturers. In fact, *Halal* implementation – covering the aspects of control, assurance and management in ensuring that products achieved *Halal* status – began in Nestlé Malaysia in the 1970s, followed by the formation in the 1980s of a *Halal* committee to oversee *Halal* standards from farm to fork for the company's worldwide operations.

This section introduces the major branding considerations that a firm needs to understand as a prerequisite to entering the Islamic market. They include defining who the *Halal* customers are, differentiating between the different categories of *Halal*, explaining the importance of innovation in *Halal*, explaining difficulties in *Halal* certification, explaining the growing importance of *Halal* logistics and differentiating between *Halal* and kosher as religious products.

Customers of *Halal*

Halal is an Arabic word that is equivalent to the English word 'lawful' and 'wholesome'. It is an all-encompassing concept which encourages a Muslim to adopt products that promote goodness in all aspects of life, safe for consumption and produced in a clean and healthy environment.

It is predicted that the market for *Halal* products will continue to grow substantially. As it grows, it is envisioned that aisles in supermarkets all over the world will be dedicated to these products, in much the same way as kosher and other ethnic products do today (Minkus-McKenna 2007). Like the products of kosher and organic industries, *Halal* products are moving into the mainstream and appealing to consumers looking for high-quality, ethical products. Some Shariah-compliant firms reveal that not all of their customers are Muslim. For example, at the Jawhara Hotels, an alcohol-free Arabian Gulf chain, 60 per cent of the clientele are non-Muslims, drawn by the hotels' serenity and family-friendly atmosphere. A quarter of the customers of Dutch-based company Marhaba, which sells cookies and chocolate, are non-Muslims (Power and Abdullah 2009).

Grocers that learn the rules guiding Muslim diets will win a loyal following. US supermarkets are selling a lot more Middle Eastern foods such as hummus and couscous these days, as more American consumers develop a taste for them. But this is just the leading edge of a trend that could result in broader and more lucrative sales for stores that get to know and serve the US Muslim market. For example, a recent research by JWT among Muslim consumers highlighted their importance as a market segment. The report describes the Muslim market as 'It's young, it's big, and it's getting bigger.' In the US, Muslims are already being described as the 'new Hispanics'. While recognition of this new target for primarily Western marketers is timely, the issue is far deeper and more complex (Minkus-McKenna 2007).

As Muslim populations grow in most countries in the world it is worthwhile for grocers in appropriate markets to adjust product assortments and marketing approaches. It is estimated that 70 per cent of Muslims worldwide follow *Halal* standards (Minkus-McKenna 2007). But before they can meet the needs of devout Muslims, grocers have to understand the dietary restrictions that dictate their purchases, and that might prove harder than it sounds. While there are some clear guidelines regarding the Muslim diet, there is no worldwide authority on *Halal*. Currently there are more than 15 *Halal* logos in the market, (Minkus-McKenna 2007).

Halal Categories

The *Halal* industry is growing in sophistication as well as size. It is no longer about just meat; it is embracing products from lipstick to vaccines to savings accounts. To illustrate, in 1990 the Islamic Food and Nutrition Council of America had only 23 clients paying for its *Halal* certification services. Last year it certified products for 2,000 companies worldwide (Power and Gatsiounis 2007).

In general, the *Halal* market can be divided into three interlinked categories: food, lifestyles and services.

FOOD

The food category is currently dominated by non-Muslim multinationals such as KFC and Nestlé although Muslim-owned manufacturers such as Al Islami brand in the United Arab Emirates and Almarai in Saudi Arabia, as well as a myriad of small local manufacturers, are growing rapidly. The lack of Arab *Halal* brands in the international marketplace is due to the fact that the concept of *Halal* food was never an issue at the Arab countries level because it was taken for granted that all food sold in these markets was *Halal*. The recognition of the significance of being *Halal* didn't evolve until the Arab markets became more open to global trade and were flooded with food products coming from non-Muslim countries which didn't have a clear understanding of the importance of the *Halal* concept to their Muslim markets.

LIFESTYLE

In the lifestyle category, which is also dominated by non-Muslim multinationals, Islamic producers of *Halal* cosmetics, i.e., those made without alcohol or animal fats, are slowly establishing their brands in the Muslim marketplace. The slow development of the *Halal* lifestyle category, in comparison to the food category, can be attributed to two factors. First, albeit important, this sector didn't have the same urgency as food. Second, both Muslims and multinationals learned late that since *Halal* actually extends beyond food, and normal day activities can also be Islamized and classified as *Halal*. Special Islamic-compliant lifestyle-related products began to be developed to meet the needs of this market and at the same time to capitalize on the opportunity it provides.

SERVICES

The services category includes finance, hospitality and logistics, among others. Of these, the *Halal* financial services are the most developed with Islamic banks controlling huge amounts of money and growing at an annual rate of nearly 15 per cent. Banks that operate according to Shariah law are doing well during the global downturn because they tend to be more conservative. In hospitality, hotels are increasingly running Islamic lines, such as Dubai's Villa Rotana, which offers quieter and more family-friendly places to stay (Anonymous 2009).

Halal Innovation

To keep growing, *Halal* firms know they cannot simply rely on religion as the driving force behind their marketing campaigns. At the end of the day, people will not buy *Halal* simply because it is *Halal*. They are going to buy quality food. Ideology doesn't make a better-tasting burger, a better car or a better computer, but it makes a powerful marketing pitch (Power and Abdullah 2009). *Halal* brands cannot stand still. In the medium term it is possible for competitors to copy those aspects that have given them the advantage. It is therefore imperative for them to innovate continuously (Melewar and Walker 2003).

New *Halal* products and services include food and non-food items and they originate in the Middle East, Europe and South East Asia. The Swiss food giant Nestlé is a pioneer in the field. It has a *Halal* committee since the 1980s, and it has long had separate facilities for its *Halal* products. As a result, the company's turnover in *Halal* products was $3.6 billion in 2008 with 75 of its 456 factories equipped for *Halal* production. For non-food items, companies like South Korea's LG and Finnish cell-phone giant Nokia also target Muslim consumers. LG provides an application that helps direct users to Mecca, while Nokia provides downloadable recitations from the Quran as well as maps of locations of major mosques in the Middle East.

Such offerings increase brand loyalty. Mainstream brands can actually appeal to Muslims without making changes to their core products; these companies can alter their marketing communications to show Muslims that their brands care about them as consumers (Power and Abdullah 2009).

Halal Certification

Halal certification assures Muslim consumers on the *Halal* status of the certified products; it confirms that the products are permissible under Islamic law. For a product to be certified it must pass inspection by an Islamic certifying agency.

Although obtaining *Halal* certification will result in changes in the production process, it can be very rewarding since Muslims comprise the largest consumer segments in the world today with a *Halal* market that is expected to reach US$2.1 trillion by 2015, not to mention the growth in the demand for *Halal* products that is spilling over to non-Muslim consumers.

The *Halal* food market has exploded in the past decade and is now worth about 16 per cent of the entire global food industry, which corresponds to $632 billion annually. If the fast-growing Islamic finance sector and the many other Islamic products and services – cosmetics, real estate, hotels, fashion, and insurance – are counted, the sector is worth nearly $1.5 trillion a year. The Islamic finance industry's value is growing at around 15 per cent a year, and could reach $4 trillion in five years, up from $500 billion today, according to a 2008 report from Moody's Investors Service (Power and Abdullah 2009).

Kosher and *Halal*

Muslims and Jews, although separated by a bloody past, a grim present and an uncertain future, are united in at least one thing: their dietary restrictions. *Halal* (Muslim) and kosher (Jewish) have significant similarities that make them interchangeable in many cases; Muslims and Jews can consume each other's foods.

Kosher and *Halal* describe an assortment of foods and beverages that are acceptable to Muslims and Jews. However, unlike kosher, which applies only to food, *Halal* is a term encompassing not only foods and drinks, but all other matters of daily life; it includes everything a Muslim does – trade, finance, entertainment, work, education, consumption, etc. Nonetheless, both of these food laws have their roots in scripture, the Bible and Torah for kosher and the Quran for *Halal*.

To be more specific, while Islam prohibits all intoxicating alcohols, liquors and wines, these are considered kosher. Thus, foods and drinks showing the kosher symbol while containing alcohol are not *Halal*. Gelatine is considered kosher by many Jews regardless of its source of origin. For Muslims, if the gelatine is prepared from non-Shariah compliant source, it becomes *Haram* (prohibited). Enzymes in cheese making are considered mere secretion according to some kashrut organizations, which makes all cheese kosher. Muslims, on the other hand, look for the source of the enzyme. If it is from pigs, it is considered *Haram*. Hence cheeses showing kosher symbols may not be *Halal* (Hussaini 1993).

Moreover, both *Halal* and kosher share a strict emphasis on cleanliness that is considered even by the non-observant as synonymous with good food, which potentially broadens the appeal of *Halal* and kosher beyond their traditional niches.

In the United States, the kosher food industry is valued at $100 billion and 90,000 kosher products, compared to about 1,000 *Halal*-certified products. Muslims' purchases account for 16 per cent of the entire US kosher food industry. On the other hand, although *Halal* products attract some Jewish consumers, Jewish purchases of *Halal* are very small by comparison (Minkus-McKenna 2007).

Challenges Facing MNCs entering Islamic Markets

BRAND ENTRY MODE

A major issue facing MNCs contemplating an entry into Islamic markets is whether to use the existing brands, create new brands designed specifically for these markets, use tester brands or use a mix of all or some of these. For example, should Nestlé introduce the same successful brands it sells outside the Muslim world unchanged, or should it brand them differently? What would make better business sense: to sell Smarties as is to Muslims or to develop a new brand of them specifically for Muslims? Should McDonalds sell Big Macs and the rest of its product range in the Arab Muslim market or should it sell MacArabia and similar Arabized brands?

The answers to these questions are not straightforward. Managing and developing a single corporate brand is far simpler and more cost-effective than managing a portfolio of country or region-specific brands. Such an international expansion of a corporate brand is bound to create economies of scale in its own right. However, there are also disadvantages in using the existing corporate brands unchanged. A company entering the Islamic market may be able to spread its risk by using a tester brand that in essence can afford to fail because the company could in theory reintroduce itself to the market with a different offering in the future. If an existing brand was used to enter that market and it failed to be accepted as Islamic, failure would damage the company's future efforts to engage that market (Melewar and Walker 2003).

COUNTRY OF ORIGIN

The country of origin of the MNC is of special importance for companies wishing to enter the Islamic market. The Muslim consumer is emotionally very sensitive due to several factors including the unity between religion and life in Islam, unlike Western consumers whose behaviours have largely evolved independent of the influence of religion due to the historical separation between state and faith in Western societies. (Although some might argue, rightfully so, that the behaviour of religious Westerners is influenced by their religion; the difference is surely that Christianity is less specific about dress, food etc. And of course many Westerners are not religious at all.) This inseparability affects Muslims' attitudes and behaviours towards products they buy and companies they deal with. For instance, all Danish companies are still stumbling from the cartoons published in a Danish newspaper several years ago because they were seen by the Muslim population as derogatory to an Islamic subject. In fact these companies faced a massive consumer boycott that resulted in serious losses for many of them. The effect of these cartoons will prevent any Danish company in the near future from establishing itself in the Islamic market, especially as there are viable alternatives to the Danish brands. Even the more established and rooted American brands face difficulties in the Muslim market during tensions between Muslim states or individuals and the United States. Melewar, an international authority on branding and brand management, warns that different nations have differing degrees of national identities. These identities not only take the form of patriotism, but they can also determine how likely a nation is to endorse the brand of a particular country. In order to understand this opportunity, the corporate brand must first understand whether the perception of nationality help or hinder it (Melewar and Walker 2003).

On the other hand some countries are perceived positively by the Muslim consumer. Switzerland, e.g., has no history of conflict with Muslims, it is the chosen place where many Muslims keep their money and spend their vacations. Being associated with a positively perceived country facilitates a company's entry into the Muslim market.

GLOBAL *HALAL* STANDARDS

Halal standards help companies and customers distinguish what is accepted from a Shariah perspective. A product can either be *Halal* or *Haram* depending on its ingredients and all the activities associated with it from the point of origin to the point of consumption and going through the entire value chain that created it. As illustrated in the case of the Australian Muslim scholars and the Australian beef industry, many of these standards remain either underdeveloped or lacking consensus. This is so due to the novelty of *Halal* and *Haram* as commercial terms and the globalization of markets which brought Muslim consumers face to face with products from non-Muslim nations that they have historically seen as adversaries. Before globalization there was no mentioning of the word '*Halal*' among Muslim consumers, aside from those travelling to non-Muslim countries, since products in the Muslim markets were produced locally or by neighbouring Muslim countries, where *Halal* was taken for granted.

The exposure to an array of foreign products resulted in a need to standardize *Halal* for the benefit of both businesses and consumers. As experience has shown, setting global *Halal* standards that firms can follow when developing products for their Islamic prospects proved to be a daunting task. The difficulty arises from the fact that the process requires that many parties must be involved, including Islamic scholars, trade experts and food scientists. These parties also don't make the job of an Islamizing firm easy with their long lists of terms and conditions, thus making the goal of becoming *Halal*-certified hard to attain. In doing so, they might be forgetting that one of the most basic teachings of the religion of Islam is that everything that Allah created is *Halal*, with minor exceptions (Power and Gatsiounis 2007). Those experts unfortunately seem to view the process the other way around; *Haram* is the rule and *Halal* is the exception.

Moreover, too many *Halal* certification agencies are being set up all over the world with some of them definitely not up to the task either because they lack the expertise or because they are not following mainstream Islam. Although the proliferation of these agencies might seem confusing to the novice Muslim market entrant, it is worth noting that there are some agencies that have the expertise, skills and regulations that qualify them as *Halal* certifiers. Basically all government-backed agencies and large Muslim groups' institutions are considered trustworthy sources by consumers and, thus, firms should strive to get their *Halal* logo certified by at least one of them, instead of getting the more risky independent certifiers who might have jumped on the *Halal* bandwagon for profiteering. Specifically, Saudi, Emirati, Sudanese and Malaysian approvals are highly regarded across the Muslim world.

Conclusion

In order to maximize their chances of success in Islamic markets, MNCs need to build branding localization competencies. In comparison to their local Muslim counterparts, multinationals generally commence with the key advantage of a higher level of managerial competence in marketing and brand building. These MNCs are equipped with sophisticated marketing and brand-building skills that are far ahead of most of their local counterparts – many of which are still struggling to master elementary distinctions such as the difference between marketing and sales (Williamson and Zeng 2004).

In spite of having the branding expertise to begin with, Western brands usually lack the cultural awareness and local knowledge needed for the successful penetration of Islamic markets (Temporal 2008). A hasty entry unequipped with the required level of awareness and knowledge will hinder or at least delay a brand's Islamic penetration. There are numerous examples to learn from in this regard. A famous drug company marketing a new remedy in the United Arab Emirates used pictures to convey its message. The first picture on the left was of someone ill, the next picture showed the person taking the medication, the final picture on the right showed a healthy person. What Arab consumers saw was a healthy person taking the remedy and then falling ill; Arabs as well as many Muslim people including Pakistan, Iran, and Afghanistan read from right to left (Alserhan 2010a). If major firms still make these mistakes one can only image what novice entrants might do.

A firm intending to enter the Islamic market has to carefully weigh the various brand entry modes available to them, namely: creating new brands, using existing brands, using tester brands or using a mix of all or some of these. The choice must be linked to the firm's corporate strategy and at the same time based on thorough understanding of the Muslim consumer, Shariah principles and the implications of the concept of *Halal* on the various organizational marketing aspects. Firms need to recognize that *Halal* status must be achieved throughout a firm's supply chain. Implementing *Halal* in some stages and excluding it in other stages will render the brand un-Islamic, not exactly the desirable outcome firms hoping to capitalize on the opportunities provided by this huge market would want to see.

Key Terms:

- Religious branding
- Islamic branding
- Islamic products
- Islamic brands
- Brand Islamization
- *Halal* logistics
- *Halal* certification
- *Halal* categories
- Ethnic brands
- Kosher brands.

References

Alserhan, B. A. (2010a) 'Entrepreneurs and trade names: evidence from the United Arab Emirates.' *European Business Review*, 22(2): c.

Alserhan, B. A. (2010b). 'Islamic branding: A conceptualization of related terms.' *Journal of Brand Management* 18: 34–49.

Anonymous (2009). 'A *Halal* shopping cart.' *Time South Pacific* (Australia/New Zealand edition) 173(20): 32–3.

Drenttel, W. (2004). 'My country is not a brand.' *Design Observer*, 25 November. Retrieved 11 September 2009, from http://www.designobserver.com/observatory/entry.html?entry=2707.

Duncan, T. and J. Ramaprasad (1995). 'Standardized multinational advertising: the influencing factors.' *Journal of Advertising* 24(3): 13.

Hussaini, M. (1993). *Islamic Dietary Concepts and Practices*. Chicago, IL: Al-Meezan International Publishing, The Islamic Food & Nutrition Council of America (IFANCA).

Jain, S. C. (1989). 'Standardization of international marketing strategy: some research hypotheses.' *Journal of Marketing Review* 53: 9.

Kustin, R. A. (2004). 'Marketing mix standardization: a cross cultural study of four countries.' *International Business Review* 13(5): 12.

Melewar, T. C. and C. M. Walker (2003). 'Global corporate brand building: Guidelines and case studies.' *Journal of Brand Management* 11(2): 157–70.

Minkus-McKenna, D. (2007). 'The pursuit of *Halal*.' *Progressive Grocer* 86(17): 42

Power, C. (2008). '*Halal* goes global.' *New Statesman* 137(4900): 18.

Power, C. and S. Abdullah (2009). 'Buying Muslim.' *Time South Pacific* (Australia/New Zealand edition) 173(20): 31–4.

Power, C. and I. Gatsiounis (2007). 'Meeting the *Halal* test.' *Forbes* 179(8): 82–5.

Temporal, P. (2008). 'Islamic branding research project announced at Saïd Business School.' Retrieved 31 October 2009 from http://www.sbs.ox.ac.uk/news/media/Press+Releases/Islamic+branding+research.htm.

Williamson, P. and M. Zeng (2004). 'Strategies for competing in a changed China.' *MIT Sloan Management Review* 45(4): 85–91.

Young, M. (2007). 'More to Islamic branding than meets the eye?' *Campaign* 23: 17.

Zakaria, N. and A.-N. Abdul-Talib (forthcoming). 'Applying Islamic market-oriented cultural model to sensitize strategies towards global customers, competitors, and environment.' *Journal of Islamic Marketing* 1(1): 20.

9

Islamic Branding 2:
Brands as Good Deeds[1]

Check list for Journey to Hell: War, Drugs and Danish Products.
A billboard in Pakistan, 2006

Learning Objectives

After reading this chapter, you should be able to:

- Understand the influence of religion on Muslim
  consumers' political and economic decisions
- Understand the Muslim consumers' motivations to boycott
- Understand the development and practice of Islamic branding
- Appreciate the vast potential of the Islamic market
- Define Islamic branding
- Understand the essence of Islamic branding.

---

1   This chapter has been previously published as Alserhan, B. A. (2010). 'On Islamic branding;
    brands as good deeds.' *Journal of Islamic Marketing* 1 (2): 101–106.

Danish Brands and the Politics of Boycotts

All Danish businesses suffered significant losses in Islamic markets when Muslim consumers boycotted their goods to protest at the publication of caricatures of the Prophet Mohammad. The drawings published by newspaper *Jyllands-Posten* in September 2006 sparked protests in Muslim countries. Islam widely holds that representations of the Prophet Mohammad are banned for fear they could lead to idolatry.

The boycott was costly to Denmark's companies and raised fears of long-term damage to the trade ties between Muslim consumers and Danish companies. These damages could go beyond exports, extending to service contracts, shipping and production facilities in the area – losses that are difficult to quantify. However, in certain industries it is possible to understand the magnitude of loss. For example, Arla Foods, one of Europe's largest dairy companies, is thought to be the worst hit, losing an estimated $1.6 million each day during the peak of the boycott.

Danish brands such as Havarti cheese, Puck, Arla, LURPAK, Hazz, ecco, Lego and many others were removed from the shelves of stores in Muslim countries around the world as Muslims awaited an apology for the offensive cartoons. The boycotts began in Saudi Arabia in January 2006 when supermarkets either put up signs saying 'stop buying Danish goods' or removed products from their shelves.

Since the boycott began in Saudi Arabia, it has spread to almost all Muslim nations. For example, a supermarket in Cairo run by France's Carrefour has signs saying that it is not offering Danish products 'in solidarity with Muslims and Egyptians'. A spokesman for Carrefour in France said the store was a franchise run by an Egyptian company. Carrefour stores run by partners and franchises are free to make commercial decisions according to their local situations. In Indonesia the importers association boycotted Danish goods. In Syria, banners on walls and storefronts all call for consumers to avoid Danish products. Employees of the Danish Lurpak butter agent in Syria raised a banner in front of their Damascus office saying: 'Yasser al-Srayyed [the agent's name] has stopped importing Lurpak.' The situation caused great concern among the members of the Confederation of Danish Industries, which represents Denmark's major companies. There was also the fear that the consumer in the future will not remember exactly what happened, but they will remember an unfavourable connection to Denmark. Such a negative association is detrimental and it is not how the Danish industries want to be perceived in Islamic markets.

A byproduct of the boycott is that some Danish companies are distancing themselves from Denmark and putting more emphasis on being international brands rather than Danish. Charlotte Simonsen, the spokeswoman for Lego, explains 'We have never marketed ourselves as a Danish product, we see ourselves as an international brand.' Such an action seems to be very important taking into consideration the feelings of Muslim consumers who believe the lines on the Pakistani billboard quoted at the beginning of this chapter.

Finally, in many supermarkets in the Islamic world, empty retail shelves with labels in English and Arabic indicate that Danish products have been withdrawn. Some commentators though have said that the shortfall may represent an opportunity for other brands, including Fonterra (New Zealand), Kraft (United States) and Nestlé (Switzerland). See *China Daily* (2006).

Introduction

The practice of Islamic branding has been gaining considerable momentum in academic circles within the past few years, both within and outside the Islamic world. The significant publicity it continues to attract, and generate, resulted in the organization of numerous high-profile events in various parts of the world, the production of journal articles and books, the formation of dedicated research groups and special projects, and at least one academic journal: the *Journal of Islamic Marketing*. In fact, the field is already experiencing a severe shortage of experts due to the ever growing worldwide demand for Islamic branding skills. Considering the length of time needed to make a branding expert and the novelty of this particular area of inquiry, one could say with certainty that this shortage is not expected to ease within the foreseeable future.

The huge demand on Islamic branding expertise, which is fuelled by the massive size of the Islamic market, the growing number of multinationals competing there and the newly emerging trend of well-financed companies from the Islamic world targeting non-Islamic markets, can only be forecasted to increase.

An additional skill-related problem that Islamic branding has to deal with is that many of those who are described as experts on Islamic branding tend to view the concept from the same perspective as conventional branding, i.e., projecting traditional branding techniques which are culturally bound onto this new and qualitatively different market. Such an approach to Islamic branding limits their ability to adequately appreciate its full context and implications.

Finally, a key obstacle facing academics and practitioners today is the lack of a precise definition that clarifies what is and what is not Islamic branding. A review of the growing, yet inadequate literature, reveals that the connotations of the concept remain overly broad; it is being used differently by different people presuming that they are using the description 'Islamic' correctly.

An Overview of the Islamic Market

The Muslim market is composed of approximately 21.01 per cent or 1.43 billion of the entire world population (CIA 2009). Muslims represent a majority in more than 50 countries in Asia, Africa and Europe and their religion, Islam, is considered the fastest growing among all religions on earth (Saeed et al. 2001). Those 1.43 billion Muslims live in economically feasible numbers in most countries in the world. The global Muslim consumer market is estimated at US$2.7 trillion today, and is forecast to reach a staggering $30 trillion by 2050 (JWT 2007).

The largest Islamic body, the Organization of the Islamic Conference (OIC), is composed of the economies of 57 member states, 50 of which are overly Muslim. The remaining members have large Muslim populations, although Muslims are not a majority in them. The percentage of Muslims in Russia, e.g., approximately stands at 15 per cent, yet Russia is a member state. India on the other hand, has a Muslim population of 150 million but its membership of the OIC is blocked by some countries due to geopolitical reasons.

Those 57 countries have a combined GDP of nearly US$8 trillion (before the oil boom of 2008). The richest country on the basis of GDP per capita is United Arab Emirates. The recent boom in oil prices has significantly increased these figures in all oil-producing Muslim countries. In 2008, Abu Dhabi, a member emirate in the United Arab Emirates, had a per capita income of US$75,000, which is double that of most European countries, and almost double the US figure.

The *Halal* market, i.e., products that are Shariah-compliant, represents a significant portion of these countries' economies. Moreover, other countries that are not members of the OIC but have feasible Muslim minorities also contribute to the global size of the *Halal* market, which is currently estimated at approximately USD 670 billion (Nestorovic 2010). Table 9.1 includes some very interesting figures that help clarify why multinationals are venturing into the *Halal* market, which is estimated to grow at 15 per cent annually making it the fast growing market in the world.

As discussed in Chapter 8, the *Halal* industry includes three main categories: (1) food, which is currently dominated by non-Muslim multinationals such as KFC and Nestlé, (2) lifestyle, which is dominated by non-Muslim multinationals, and (3) services, including finance, hospitality and logistics, among others. Islamic services, especially finance, are currently dominated by Muslims, although this might change as more major countries and regions, notably China and Europe, develop an interest.

Table 9.1   **Size of the *Halal* market**

Region value	Muslim population (Million)	Halal food market US$ (Million)
South Central Asia	653	210,000
Africa	491	144,250
West Asia	195	116,850
South East Asia	236	97,300
Europe (including Russia)	51	63,750
China	130	22,925
North America	7.1	12,425
South America	3.1	1,550
Oceania	0.6	900
TOTAL	1,766.80	669,950

Source: Adopted from Nestorovic (2010)

What is Islamic Branding?

Until now, there seems to be no clear understanding of what the term 'Islamic branding' means, a situation that sometimes leads to using the term 'Islamic' in a rather insensitive manner. For example, when the term is used to describe products originating in Islamic countries one would conclude that wines produced there are Islamic just because of the location of their production. Consequently, wines produced in Tunisia, Turkey, Egypt and Jordan can be rightly described as *Halal*, or Islamic.

To avoid such confusion and reduce the likelihood of improper use, the term 'Islamic branding' is analyzed in this chapter according to its scope and how it has been used. To clarify, the term 'Islamic brand' could be used to describe brands as 'Islamic' because (1) these brands are Shariah-compliant, i.e., *Islamic brands by religion*, (2) they originate from an Islamic country, i.e., *Islamic brands by country of origin*, or (3) their target is the Muslim consumer, i.e., *Islamic brands by destination* (Alserhan, 2010a). As shown in Figure 9.1, the combination of these three descriptions of Islamic brands creates four distinct types of brands: true Islamic brands, traditional Islamic brands, inbound Islamic brands and outbound Islamic brands.

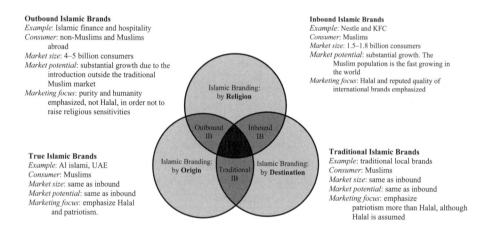

Outbound Islamic Brands
Example: Islamic finance and hospitality
Consumer: non-Muslims and Muslims abroad
Market size: 4–5 billion consumers
Market potential: substantial growth due to the introduction outside the traditional Muslim market
Marketing focus: purity and humanity emphasized, not Halal, in order not to raise religious sensitivities

True Islamic Brands
Example: Al islami, UAE
Consumer: Muslims
Market size: same as inbound
Market potential: same as inbound
Marketing focus: emphasize Halal and patriotism.

Inbound Islamic Brands
Example: Nestle and KFC
Consumer: Muslims
Market size: 1.5–1.8 billion consumers
Market potential: substantial growth. The Muslim population is the fast growing in the world
Marketing focus: Halal and reputed quality of international brands emphasized

Traditional Islamic Brands
Example: traditional local brands
Consumer: Muslims
Market size: same as inbound
Market potential: same as inbound
Marketing focus: emphasize patriotism more than Halal, although Halal is assumed

Islamic Branding: by Religion

Outbound IB   Inbound IB

Islamic Branding: by Origin   Traditional IB   Islamic Branding: by Destination

Figure 9.1   Categories of Islamic branding

1.   *True Islamic brands*. These brands satisfy the three descriptions of Islamic branding; they are *Halal*, produced in an Islamic country, and they target Muslim consumers. The word 'true' which is used here doesn't mean that the other categories of Islamic branding are 'wrong'. For example, the vast majority of the brands that originate from Islamic countries are *Halal*, simply because they were intended for the Muslim consumer in the first place.

2.   *Traditional Islamic brands*. Brands originating in Islamic countries and targeting Muslims. As explained above, these are assumed to be *Halal*. Prior to the globalization of Islamic markets, it was taken for granted that all brands available there were *Halal*.

3.   *Inbound Islamic brands*. *Halal* brands that target Muslim consumers but originate from non-Islamic countries. These brands were mostly Islamized, i.e., changed in order to make them *Halal*.

4.   *Outbound Islamic brands*. *Halal* brands that originate from Islamic countries but do not necessarily target Muslim consumers.

The Essence of Islamic Branding

Attempting to understand and approach the concept and practice of Islamic branding in the traditional sense of branding will deprive firms of real business opportunities within the attractive Islamic market. This market, which is growing exponentially, is drawing both Muslims who want to practise their religion correctly and non-Muslims who are motivated by the simplicity, purity and humanity that Islamic brands are assumed to embody.

For Muslims, branding cannot be separated from faith, which dictates that all actions should be divine and that one loves and hates not because of his human desires but because his feelings are in line with Allah's guidance. Trade relationships, e.g., even though they result in the satisfaction of earthly desires, should be forged with a divine intent between business parties. Hence, the entire relationship ceases to be of a materialistic nature and transforms into a good deed that will be noted in the divine record of each individual. What makes Islamic branding different is that manufacturers do not manufacture objects, they manufacture righteousness; sellers do not sell objects and things, they invite into a righteous life; and buyers do not buy necessities and material comfort, they engage in worship. Such an understanding gives Islamic branding greater impetus and makes it much more powerful in connecting with customers than traditional branding.

Islamic branding is about blending the religious with the materialistic and the heavenly with the worldly. It is about religiously integrating the brand into the lives of adherents, where it is incubated and lived with the sure anticipation of Godly rewards. In Islam, all actions are judged by their underlying motive or the intention behind them. Thus all actions and motions undertaken by a Muslim, if motivated by a pure intention become good deeds regardless of their outcomes. With the right intentions, things as simple as breathing, eating and washing, among numerous other activities, become good deeds that please Allah and warrant His satisfaction (Saeed et al. 2001). Thus, when a Muslim rejects a *Haram* product or consumes a *Halal* one, it will count towards his good deeds. For example, eating healthy food is doubly rewarding for Muslims who, in addition to the prospect of a good health enjoyed by everyone, get the extra reward of knowing that they are complying with the teachings of their religion. The same example applies to almost all types of consumption and consumables. While non-Muslim consumers can be allured by the apparent benefits which can be easily realized within a relatively short time period, Muslims' consumption is driven by a second yet more potent factor, i.e., doing a good deed. Thus if brand A of water is more Islamic than brand B then Muslims are to actively adopt the first and *actively* neglect the second. Brands endorsed by religion become good deeds and that is what all brands that target the Muslim consumer should strive to do.

Islam is not only about *Halal* and *Haram*, as commonly understood by Muslim and non-Muslim branding experts who are either not well-versed in the related Islamic teachings or view them from an abstract perspective, i.e., *Halal* and *Haram*. Moreover, many of those experts fail to appreciate the basic Islamic fact that *Halal* is the norm and *Haram* is the exception., which literally means that the majority of the things that Allah created and taught people about are created *Halal*; it is what people themselves do that transforms them into *Haram*. To illustrate, grapes are commanded in the Quran as fruits from paradise. However, processing them into intoxicating drinks makes them *Haram*. The Internet is *Halal* but using it to exchange or disseminate pornography and hatred is *Haram*. Cutting down a tree to build a house to shelter a family is *Halal* but cutting it down to build a summer house that will remain vacant most of the year is extravagance.

In particular, non-Muslim branding experts have difficulty differentiating between living Islam and having some knowledge about it and, thus, many of their branding consultations fall short of appreciating the depth of a brand ingrained in religion. It is not difficult to memorize the few items that are considered *Haram* in Islam. In fact, it doesn't take an expert to say that Islam prohibits the consumption of wine, but it takes one to appreciate the strength of the general Muslim public's feelings towards wine consumption. To illustrate, I was once invited to a dinner in the UK with a group of people who were supposed to be among the very few experts in the western hemisphere on Islamic branding. While they were discussing the potential of Islamic brands they were sipping wine. The point to be made here is that brands are strongly attached to emotions and their success depends on living, or at least feeling, them. In addition to abstract knowledge, they require passion, sincerity and honesty; discussing them from a purely academic perspective means depriving them of their soul. Sipping wine, dining on pork and discussing Islamic brands is certainly non-Islamic and that is probably why Western expertise, despite leading the branding efforts in the Islamic world for the last several decades, has so far failed to produce the long anticipated wave of Islamic super-brands; they failed to live these brands because the underlying motivation for their branding efforts are commercial, the descriptor 'good deeds' is absent. What many experts see, including Muslims, is an opportunity for commercial gain, not one that has the potential to add an ethical dimension to the prevailing branding practices.

Although branding to Muslims could make use of the branding techniques developed by Western experts, it has to take into consideration the spiritual needs of the target Muslim consumers. For Muslims, who are growing ever more spiritual, all actions are integrated and all actions are either pleasing or displeasing to Allah. Thus, they are careful about what, when, where, how, from whom and how much to consume. Marketers could easily forget this long chain of interrelated questions and issues to consider and thus risk alienating their Muslim customers. In fact, as noted earlier, Muslims are intrinsically motivated to actively boycott brands that seem to be in violation of some of the teachings of Islamic. The word actively means encouraging others to boycott as well. For example, a majority of Muslim customers who are aware of the Danish brands say that the quality and the price of these brands are competitive, if not superior. However; many Muslims stopped buying them throughout the Muslim world because they were actively branded as *bad deeds*, a sin; no one wants to be seen sinning! Being branded as a bad deed among Muslim consumers is a marketer's nightmare.

Key Terms:

- Islamic branding
- Good deeds
- *Halal* market
- *Halal* industry
- True Islamic brands
- Traditional Islamic brands
- Inbound Islamic brands
- Outbound Islamic brands
- Marketing focus
- Purity
- Humanity
- Branding consultations.

References

Alserhan, B. A. (2010a) 'Entrepreneurs and trade names: evidence from the United Arab Emirates.' *European Business Review* 22(2): c.

Alserhan, B. A. (2010b). 'Islamic branding: A conceptualization of related terms.' *Journal of Brand Management* 18: 34–49.

China Daily (2006) 'Muslim boycotts of Danish products costly.' 17 February 09:12. Retrieved June 2010 from http://www.chinadaily.com.cn/english/doc/2006-02/17/content_521276.htm.

CIA (2009). *The World Factbook.* Washington, DC: CIA.

JWT (2007) Study reveals one of America's biggest hidden niche markets. New York. Retrieved 19 February 2011 from http://muslimadnetwork.com/archives/jwt-study-reveals-one-of-americas-biggest-hidden-niche-markets.

Nestorovic, C. (2010) Trends in the European Halal Business. Seminar at the United Arab Emirates University.

Saeed, M., Ahmed, Z. U. and Mukhtar, S.-M. (2001) 'International marketing ethics from an Islamic perspective: a value-maximization approach.' *Journal of Business Ethics* 32: 127–42.

10

Islamic Hospitality

Whoever believes in Allah and the Last Day should be hospitable with his guest.

Prophet Mohammad

The Luthan Hotel & Spa is the first hotel in Saudi Arabia where women can publicly attend conference, swim, dine or use the gym anytime they please. All staff at the Luthan are female, from director to porters. Hotels like Luthan are growing in the region.

Thomas 2008

Learning Objectives

After reading this chapter, you should be able to understand and describe:

- The relationship between Islamic hospitality and Islamic tourism
- The relationship between Arab hospitality and Islamic hospitality
- Islam's view of customers: guests not customers
- The status of guests in Islam
- The scope of Islamic hospitality
- The market for Islamic hospitality
- The requirements of Islamic hospitality
- The challenges facing Islamic hospitality.

Halal Holidays in the Sun[1]

Muslim women can often be seen swimming while veiled – though they may not want to on beaches where most women are wearing bikinis. The problem also occurs in some resorts in Muslim countries with an international tourist trade. Expensive hotels in some Arab countries actually ban veiled women from their pools so that Western guests feel at home. One answer for Muslim families who want to play in the water together is *Halal* tourism.

The idea took off several years ago, as hotel companies witnessed the success of the Shariah-compliant banking and investment sector and saw their opportunity. It encompasses the main aspects of Shariah-compliant living such as alcohol abstinence, *Halal* food, separate mosques for prayer and modest dressing. And with nearly 1.6 billion Muslims in the world, the potential market is huge.

Mizan Raja, his wife Nazma Begum and their four children travelled this summer from the UK to Alanya, on Turkey's southern, Mediterranean coast, for a beach holiday. They had been to British resorts before – such as Brighton and Southend-on-Sea – but Nazma could only watch while the others played. 'I really thought I was missing out to be honest, like I was held back from doing something that was really fun and enjoyable. But here, everybody has been getting involved and having lots of fun,' she said.

WOMEN-ONLY FACILITIES

Large screens in the reception area of the family's four-star hotel advertised the hotel's facilities, without using female models. Between enjoying the beach, the restaurants, the segregated spa facilities and pool areas, guests hear the call to prayer five times a day.

Another feature that many women consider the highlight is an open-air women-only swimming pool on the sixth floor, at the very top of the hotel. Even the elevator accessing the pool is for women alone.

Before Nazma and I got into the pool we were both checked for cameras and mobile phones. Nazma's experience of women-only pools in England was quite different, she said. 'I've actually been to a women-only pool session and all of a sudden a man walked in and he was going to be the lifeguard, which

---

1   This section is by Shaimaa Khalil, reporter for BBC World News travel show Fast Track.

contradicted what it was all about,' she said. A remarkable thing about the women-only pool area is how relaxed the women look. Most of the women in the hotel were covered. They either wore a headscarf (hijab) or full-face veil (niqab).

In the ladies' pool, however, none of the women were covered, and some were wearing regular swimming costumes. 'One person, the other day, I didn't recognise her!' Nazma said. 'She was wearing the burkini [an Islamic bikini] but she looked so different because she [normally] wears the niqab. I could see her face and she was smiling. You could tell she felt safe and secure in this environment,' Nazma added.

GROWING MARKET

On the beach I met Thuraya Al Haj Mustafa, a Palestinian-German who has been coming to Turkey with her family for the past five years. They were one of the first families to try the *Halal* beach holidays. 'What I enjoy myself is being able to go to the beach with my whole family, not just my husband, to go to the sea. I can go as well. I can swim with my children,' she said. 'I can have fun with them. You know in Arab countries like Palestine its normal for ladies to sit by the beach but not to swim. Here I can do everything I like,' Thuraya said.

With countries like Turkey, Malaysia and Indonesia leading the way in *Halal* tourism, the Middle East has yet to exploit this young, growing market. Dubai-based Almulla Hospitality, e.g., recently unveiled plans for a Shariah-compliant brand, comprising of 30 hotels, and targeting Saudi Arabia, the United Arab Emirates, Jordan, Egypt and Malaysia. By 2013, Almulla wants to have 150 properties worldwide – including 35 in Europe – and plans to spend over $2 billion to reach its goal but there has been no news of its development Only a handful of Shariah or *Halal* hotel developments have so far materialized in the region – yet the World Tourism Organisation says Gulf travellers spend $12 billion (£7.7 billion) annually on leisure travel.

Abdul Sahib Al Shakiry, an Iraqi tourism expert and founder of *Islamic Tourism Magazine*, said that a good chunk of this money could be channelled into the *Halal* tourism industry. 'People want to spend money and if you give them what they want, they'll spend money in this direction and there will be business,' he said. But while some welcome the arrival of the Islamic beach holiday, others see it as a form of isolationism.

'DOUBLE STANDARDS'

'I find it very alarming,' says Muslim writer and columnist Yasmin Alibhai-Brown. 'Cultural racism or religious racism, which is what this to me is, is saying there is no common humanity. That we have to, even on holiday, be apart from the rest of you. 'You can go on holiday anywhere in the world and you don't have to drink, nobody forces you to drink.' I accept the *Halal* food argument but there are always other things you can eat. 'How would we feel if there were Christian –White only holidays advertised?' she said. 'We would be appalled. You can't have double standards.'

Thuraya, on the other hand, said that such holidays are not isolating but rather bring people together. 'You see Muslim people from all over the world. You have Muslim people from China, Russia, Belgium, and France. 'The other thing is that when I go to any other normal vacation or hotel they wouldn't accept me wearing the burkini,' she added. 'They don't make me feel comfortable so why should I go there? I'm not searching for isolation but there's no other possibility for me as a Muslim lady,' she said.

Whether or not *Halal* tourism drives people apart, or brings them together, one thing is for sure – Mizan, Nazma and their children had a fantastic time on this beach holiday.

On their last day in Alanya, Nazma told me that the one thing that has given her a sense of freedom she had not had before is the burkini. 'I'm not held back any more. I've been able to go in the sea and take part and not think twice. Everyone I've seen has been wearing burkinis, so I don't feel like the odd one out. It's been a really good experience and something that we want to come back and enjoy next year.'

Introduction

Islamic hospitality is a thriving sector that is attracting significant attention and investment. The sector, which reflects a new trend in the hospitality industry in the Islamic world, focuses on the adoption of business practices and finance based on the Islamic principles of Shariah. This trend is developing rapidly and becoming more diverse since it is no longer associated only with religious tourism. Its latest manifestation is the development of fully fledged Shariah-compliant hotels and facilities in many places around the world, not just Mecca and Medina in Saudi Arabia. These hotels provide a competitive range of services rivalling those provided by traditional Western-style hotels.

Although these hotels are being branded primarily as either dry hotels or Islamic hotels, their customers come from different cultural and religious backgrounds. While the religious appeal is effective in attracting Muslims, attracting Western tourists is based on motivations to travel that associated with well-being, conscious-lifestyles, and cultural appreciation (Stephenson et al. 2010).

Even though one might contend that these hotels – Islamic hotels – have long existed in Saudi Arabia, it can easily be argued that the Saudi hotels were dry hotels, not specifically Islamic hotels; those hotels didn't exhibit the Islamic hospitality experience, they merely operated according to the governmental regulations which ban alcohol, nightclubs and mixing in public. The spirit of an Islamic hotel was lacking in them, they were money-making hotels, not true Islamic guest houses where guests are honoured because they are guests rather than because of the size of their pockets or because of the power of their sponsoring organizations.

The new wave of Islamic hotels are different, they are Islamic because they have made a conscious choice to be so. It is true that their owners have recognized an opportunity but it is also equally true that their approach to capturing that opportunity is more professional than their rather archaic predecessors whose Islamic hospitality model was underdeveloped. This new generation of hotels aims to position and brand themselves as Islamic experience providers, not *Halal* hotels, *Halal* being only part of that experience. Having a room with a Qibla sign, a prayer rug, a bidet or an arch in the room is certainly not enough for that experience to be considered authentically Islamic. An Islamic hospitality experience must embrace the Islamic notions of hospitality in relation to congeniality and respect to visitors (Al-Hamarneh and Steiner 2004) and relates to principles embedded in the Quran emphasizing the absolute importance of being a good host (Din 1989).

The Islamic principles of hospitality which embraced many of the pre-Islamic Arab hospitality traditions apply not only to hotels but to all areas where customers are present including educational institutions, hospitals and sports facilities, to name only a few. From this perspective the expansion and growth possibilities for this sector become endless as they no longer remain primarily restricted to hotels. Having said that, it should be understood that the Islamic hotel business by itself is vast enough to warrant the huge funds planned for investment in it until the year 2020 when it is expected to fully mature and parallel its Western-style counterparts.

Arab Hospitality before Islam

Pre-Islamic Arab society attained and nurtured legendary levels of hospitality and generosity to guests unparalleled throughout history anywhere else. Arabs have gone, and continue to go, to extremes to please their guests and earn their satisfaction. When Islam came and Arabs became Muslims these traits were endorsed by the religion and made good deeds that bring a Muslim closer to Allah, the Most Generous and the Giver.

Arab historians recounted numerous incidents of Arabs competing to honour their guests. For example, the following story is narrated about the man who is known as the most generous Arab that ever lived, Hatim Al-ta'e (lived around the end of the Days of Ignorance, about AD 590). Hatim was questioned:

> 'Have you come across any one more generous than yourself?'

> Hatim replied: 'Yes, I have.'

> Hatim was asked: 'Where?'

> Hatim said: 'I had been travelling in the desert when I came across a tent. Inside it there was an old lady while behind the tent a goat lay tied. When the old lady saw me she approached me and held the reins of my horse so that I could dismount. A little later, her son arrived and was immensely pleased to have me as their guest. The old lady said to him: "Commence the preparations to entertain our guest. Go and slaughter the goat and prepare some food."

> 'The son said: "First I shall go and collect some firewood," but the old lady said: "Going to the desert and bringing the firewood shall consume a lot of time due to which our guest would have to remain hungry for long, and this would be contrary to social etiquette."

'The son, breaking the only two lances he had, slaughtered the goat, prepared, and presented the food. When I asked about their condition, I realized that the goat had been their only possession and yet, they had slaughtered it for me. I said to the old lady: "Do you recognize me?" She said no, I said: "I am Hatim Al-Ta'e. You must come with me to my tribe so that I can entertain you and shower you with gifts and presents."

'The old lady said: "Neither do we seek any reward from our guests nor do we sell bread for money," and she refused to accept anything from me. Witnessing this generosity, I realized that they were far more generous and munificent than me.

EZsoftech n.d.

Arabs even named the dog 'the voice of consciousness' and 'the creator of reputation' because it attracts guests by barking and helps them locate hosts. Moreover, when it was too windy to light a fire at night dogs were dispersed and tied around the neighbourhood so that guests would be guided by their noise to the camp. Until this day, the most generous man of a Bedouin community will place his tent on the right side of the camp; and that is how guests know to whom they should go.

The Status of Customers in Islam: Customers as Guests

The religious view of the customer as a guest is central to the conduct of Islamic hospitality. In Islam a guest is to be treated with the utmost respect whether he is an acquaintance or a stranger. In fact, being generous to a guest is associated with believing in Allah and in the Last Day, which are two of the five pillars of faith (Iman) in Islam; To believe in: Allah, His angels, His books, His messengers, and the Last Day (Day of Judgment). The prophet says: 'He who believes in Allah and in the last day let him be generous to his guest.' Although not being generous to one's guests will not render a person a non-believer, the teachings of the Prophet demonstrates the importance of giving proper care and attention to guests through linking hospitality directly to with faith.

The implication of this association is that in order to practise a higher level of faith and become an ever better Muslim, a Muslim's faith must be reflected in everything he does from removing harm from other's ways and honouring guests, all the way through to martyrdom.

Guest Treatment in Islam

Islam teaches that guests are to be well treated and to the best of a host's resources and abilities. There are many Quranic and prophetic teachings in this regards that specify the general guidelines that underlie such treatment in terms of duration, sustenance, place, manners, greetings and tenderness:

DURATION

Although there is no upper limit for how long a guest is to be treated as a guest, all guests are entitled to a minimum of 24 hours of preferential treatment in terms of services provided. Nonetheless, after the minimum period is concluded the guest continues to be honoured, as a good deed by the host: 'Whoever believes in Allah and the Last Day let him be generous to his neighbour. Whoever believes in Allah and the Last Day *let him be generous to his guest in what he gives.*' A man said, '*And what should he give O Messenger of Allah*' He replied, '*A day and a night, and one must honour his guest for three days. Whoever does more then it is a charity for him.* And whoever believes in Allah and the Last Day let him speak fair or stay quiet' (Prophet Mohammad).

CUISINE

The preferential treatment of guests includes serving the best available food that a host can afford: 'There is no person like a person who takes the reins [of his horse] and fights for the sake of Allah, avoiding people's evil, *and a person among his sheep in the outskirts giving meal to his guest, honouring his right*' (Prophet Mohammad).

PLACE

The Hadith above also indicates that hospitality should be provided where it is needed most. The value of the services provided by a host located in close proximity to many other hosts is not as valuable as those provided by a lone or a few hosts in underserviced areas, e.g., city outskirts.

GOOD MANNERS

Islam places supreme importance on the cultivation of good manners and noble moral qualities. There are many prophetic teachings in this regard: 'The best of you are those who possess the best manners', 'On the Day of Recompense nearest to me will be one who displays in one's daily life the best of manners', 'On the Day of Reckoning the most weighty item in the "Balance of Deeds" will be good manners', and once a Companion asked the Prophet, 'What is there that takes a Muslim to Paradise?' The Prophet replied, 'Fear of God and good manners.'

Islam has also described the manner in which a person should meet his guests. These include, among others, cheerfulness and sincerity. '*And your smiling in the face of your brother is charity*, your removing of stones and thorns from people's paths is charity, and your guiding a man gone astray in the world is charity for you'(Prophet Mohammad).

Muslims have also been warned against bad manners and are taught to cultivate all good and noble moral and social qualities and to avoid everything that is mean or wicked (Nomani n.d.). The Prophet said: 'A man with bad manners and a bad moral conduct shall not enter Paradise', and 'No sin is more detestable to God than bad manners.'

GREETING

Islamic hospitality, aside from being associated with faith, is also associated with the finer points of Islamic lifestyle traditions. One of the most basic of these traditions is the Islamic greeting of *as-salaamu 'alaikum* (God's Peace be upon you). 'When you are greeted with a greeting, greet with better than it or return it. Allah takes count of all things' (Quran 4:86). This greeting, although seemingly of a simple nature, has protocols specifying its use. 'The rider should salute the walker, the walker the sitter, and the few the many' (Prophet Mohammad). Finally, the Islamic greeting is not composed only of words but also shaking hands, which is encouraged as blessed and rewarded. 'When two Muslims shake hands, their sins fall to the ground, as leaves of the tree fall to the ground' (Prophet Mohammad).

TENDERNESS

Tenderness and the readiness to oblige and to put others at ease are all virtues of the highest order in the Islamic pattern of morality (Nomani n.d.). 'Hell's fire is forbidden for those that are mild and gentle and make it easy for others to deal with them.'

'God is compassionate and likes compassion in His creatures. He grants more to the kind and the tender-hearted than to those that are harsh and severe.'

GENTLENESS OF SPEECH

In Islam, gentleness of speech is a virtue and rudeness is a sin (Nomani n.d.). 'Speak fair to the People' (Quran 2:83). 'To speak politely is piety and a kind of charity', 'To indulge in intemperate language and in harsh behaviour is to perpetrate an injustice and the home of injustice is Hell', and 'Rudeness in speech is hypocrisy (i.e., the quality of a hypocrite).'

On the other hand, the guest is expected to be considerate to his host's circumstances, not burdening him with what he cannot afford. A guest should not exploit his prescribed rights because he too has prescribed duties. The Prophet said: 'It is unlawful for a Muslim to stay with his brother until he makes him fall into sin.' The companions said, 'O Messenger of Allah, how can he (the guest) make him (the host) fall into sin?' He replied, 'That he stays with him while he does not have [enough money] to serve him food.'

To conclude, the following paragraph from Imam Ghazali's book, 'Ihyaa 'Uloom-ud-Deen' (i.e., *Revival of Religious Sciences*) sheds some light on how Prophet Mohammad treated his guests:

> *The Messenger of Allah would honor his guests. He would even spread his garment for a non-relative guest to sit. He used to offer his guest his own cushion and insist until they accept it. No one came to him as a guest but thought that he was the most generous of people. He gave each one of his companions sitting with him his due portion of his attention. He would direct his listening, speech, gaze and attention to those who were in his company. Even then, his gathering was characterized by modesty, humbleness and honesty. He would call his companions by their Kunyah – the name they are known by to others – to honour them.*

Definition and Scope of Islamic Hospitality

Currently Islamic hospitality is defined as one that caters to the needs of Muslim travellers, tourists, vacationers, holiday goers and businesspeople who look for a family-friendly, tranquil, entertaining, and culturally sensitive and experience-enriching hotel. Although the use of the term is being, for now, limited to the development of Islamic hotels, its scope is much broader and includes other areas such as catering, hospitals, and most other services' businesses. In fact it includes each single encounter between people, whether business-related or otherwise. For example:

1. Islamic hospitals were established in the Middle East much earlier than hotels; the Islamic Hospital in Amman, Jordan, went into operation in 1982.

2. Most educational institutions and many universities in the Arabian Gulf have gender-based facilities where male and female students do not mix anywhere in the campus.

3. The airline catering industry has long catered to the needs of Muslim travellers by serving *Halal* meals.

4. Gender-based gyms and coffee-shops are also proliferating in many Muslim countries.

5. Female-only entertainment and folklore bands exist.

6. There are all-female-operated jewellery stores.

7. Female chauffeur services are available.

Although one might argue that many of these services traditionally fall outside the hospitality domain, the way they operate, and especially their front-stage employees, are engaged in what might be rightly described as hospitality activities, and more so, Islamic hospitality activities. Islamic hospitality, which is based on being kind, honest, hospitable and merciful to everyone whom a Muslim meets, raises the status of a client, any client, from a customer to a guest; a guest to the company's premises and facilitations whether that guest is an actual or a virtual guest in the company's cyberspace.

The Market for Islamic Hospitality

Director to porter, the Luthan Hotel in Riyadh employs only females. The hotel demonstrates the trend of emerging demand for hotels that accommodate the needs of a Muslim clientele. It also denotes the growing interest from Shariah-compliant investment funds in the booming regional tourism industry where Muslim investors controlling seemingly infinite liquidity are following their principles (Thomas 2008). Such a principled attitude to investment represents a generous opportunity for Shariah financers. Although how much of this opportunity can be translated into actual demand for Islamic hotels is difficult to determine, it is argued that demand is enough to satisfy one-third of the new hotels being constructed in the Gulf Cooperation Council (GCC). This is so because demand for these Islamic hotel services is no longer coming only from the rich in the Muslim world. Overall, Muslims are travelling more, on business and on holiday, and they want principled hotels during their travel. Hotels that target this new niche include Sharjah's Coral International, Flora Group of Dubai, Grand Seraj Hotels & Resorts, Rotana's Rayhaan, KM Holdings' Tamani Hotel, and Almulla Hospitality which is planning to invest $2 billion in creating the world's first and largest Shariah-compliant international hotel chain.

In total, these projects are planning hundreds of new Islamic hotels around the globe to tap into the rising regional demand from GCC citizens travelling abroad, which the World Trade Organization estimates at $12 billion per year. By 2020 there will be 900 new hotels worth $1 trillion (Thomas 2008).

Although these hotels are trying to position themselves as culturally sensitive Arab and Islamic hospitality brands created using Shariah-compliant funds, no brand has successfully achieved that status yet. That is of course, aside from the Mecca and Medina brands in Saudi Arabia that are being developed solely for religious tourism; their brand targets customers in these two cities and there are no plans to capitalize on their brand equity and expand anywhere else.

While the immediate target for investments in Islamic hotels seems to be the Muslim clientele, particularly observant families from the Gulf, middle-class Muslims who are travelling more, and non-Muslim travellers are also being approached. The increase in the demand from Muslims is due, among other factors, to the increased self-awareness among Muslims who are shying away from travelling to the ever more family-hostile Western environment and searching for the more peaceful and surprisingly thrilling and diverse alternative within the Islamic countries. To quote a prominent Muslim writer, Naseem Javid: 'The West's constant scrutiny of Muslims around the world has now created an unstoppable awareness among Muslims to recreate and redefine their identity, manage their affairs, and establish their own standards' (Javed 2007). As the example at the beginning of this chapter illustrates, instead of travelling to Europe where a Muslim family will be exposed to severe cultural differences, travelling to Dubai, Malaysia, Turkey or Saudi Arabia provides Muslim families with the much needed feeling of security and tranquillity.

While the religious affiliation of Islamic hotels plays a major promotional factor when selling to Muslims, non-Muslim travellers are attracted by the appeal of a culturally different approach to hospitality and a sense of peace and humanity that are lacking in the Western model of hotels where the concept of hospitality has lost much of its content due to cultural issues, rigorous profit-seeking and severe budget cuts.

Shariah Compliance Rules for Islamic Hotels

Investors in the Islamic hospitality sector, which is beginning to mature, have 'suddenly' come to recognize the fact that Muslim travellers represent approximately 10 per cent of the huge global travel market and that Muslims travel, like everybody else. However, Muslim travellers are different. They are deeply guided by a comprehensive set of religious rules and guidelines that specify how, when and where many of their activities should be carried out. As such, Islamic hospitality, in addition to assuring Muslim clients that the food is *Halal* without their having to ask and that all hotel operations are Shariah-compliant, there are numerous related activities that enhance the image of the hotel as an Islamic hotel. These activities are not necessarily classified as *Halal* or *Haram*; they are part of fine touches of the Islamic lifestyle.

One of the most comprehensive lists of these fine touches that signify the Islamic identity of the hotel has been provided by Almulla Hospitality. The company which claims that 'Our brand proposition is so distinct that guests will be confident that our brand values have universal consistency' is one of the most important investors in the field of Islamic hospitality. According to Almulla, the common rules that must be adhered to by a hotel to classify as Islamic include, but are not limited to, the following:

1. Islamic finance. Islamic hotels should be financed from funds compliant with Shariah regulations and part of the revenue must be contributed in the form of Zakat (obligatory charity) (Bakr 2008).

2. Markers indicating direction of Mecca. Markers should be placed in hotel rooms because Muslims must face Mecca every time they

pray. These markers can be placed on the ceiling, the walls, the floor, or any other object within the room. Basically these markers are basic black or green arrows with the word Qibla (Mecca) written beside them. This is not a Shariah requirement but a faith associated augmenter of the core service provided by the Islamic hotel.

3.   No alcohol to be served on the premises. It is widely known that Islam doesn't tolerate the alcohol-related consumption business. This substance can be used for industrial purposes but cannot be consumed at a personal level. A hotel that sells alcohol will not be considered an Islamic hotel.

4.   *Halal* food must be served; no pork allowed. What applies to alcoholic beverages applies to pork and pork-based products; an Islamic hotel cannot serve pork even to its non-Muslim clients and those clients should not order it in the first place. Even if the *Halal* food is isolated from pork and any other food which is not Shariah-compliant, the hotel cannot be called Islamic. An Islamic hotel prepares and serves one type of food only and that is *Halal*. For more details concerning what food and other substances are *Halal* refer to Chapter 3.

5.   Special entertainment but no nightclubs. Unfortunately, in the minds of many Muslims and non-Muslims, the words 'Muslims' and 'entertainment' do not come together due to misinterpretation of Islam by Muslims and incorrect cultural and religious stereotyping by others. Yet, one of the most significant but misunderstood Islamic concepts is the role of entertainment in living a balanced life. Entertainment in Islam is not only permitted, it is endorsed. Imam Ali, the fourth Muslim caliph, said: 'The believer's time has three periods: the period when he is in communion with Allah, the period when he manages for his livelihood, and the period when he is free to enjoy what is lawful and pleasant. And the last part is an energizer and refreshing for the other parts.'

Entertainment is an important component of the personality of the Muslim and it is one of his religious duties. The Prophet said: 'Entertain your hearts, an hour and an hour' which means that time should be dedicated to entertainment in the same way time is dedicated for pure acts of worship. Such entertainment takes many forms. For example, the Prophet teaches: 'Teach your children archery, swimming, and horse riding.'

Islamic hoteliers should be flexible and creative in providing good lawful entertainment. Besides swimming, archery and horse-riding, entertainment could include lively competitions among guests, watching movies and reading books that do not portray indecency, family games, poetry and Islamic music, painting and drawing etc. 'Passing time is easy, whether it is spent basking in the calm atmosphere, taking a dip in one of the pools – away from prying eyes – or sipping on a refreshing fruit cocktail' (Bakr 2008). On the other hand, gambling, music, wine, sculpting, female-based entertainment and indecent performances are forbidden in Islam (Jaffery 2009).

6.   Staff to be predominantly Muslim. Muslim employees are better equipped to understand the needs and cultural sensitivities of the Muslim clientele. In addition to the little training that will be needed to sensitize Muslim staff, their presence provides stronger assurance to Muslim clientele on the identity and services offered in the hotel.

7.   Male staff for single men and female staff for women and families. Muslim men tend to be very jealous and sensitive when it comes to who the female members of their families are exposed to. Even in hotels and places that are not necessarily Islamic many Muslim families will ask specifically for a waitress not a waiter to serve them.

8.   Separate male and female wellness facilities such as gyms. Islam takes a very strong view on mixing between genders and takes many precautions to ensure that unwarranted mixing does not occur, for fear of what that might lead to. In these facilities, both men and women wear clothes that are tight, short or revealing, dress characteristics that are unaccepted in the Islamic code of dress. Moreover, Muslims generally, both men and women, are not as comfortable mixing in public as others and thus many will just opt out and not use these facilities, eventually reducing their contribution to the guest's Islamic hospitality experience.

9.   Gender-segregated prayer rooms. The Islamic prayer includes certain moves, positions and postures which women cannot perform freely in the presence of men. Prayer rooms are places where peace of mind is sought and thus all distractions must be eliminated, including the distraction of men! Also, these rooms represent secluded nearby getaways where women can pray, chat and get acquainted easily with all other women in the hotel regardless of who they are or where they come from because, in these rooms, all people are equal, there are no ranks and no social classes.

10. Conservative TV channels. There are more than 60 dedicated Islamic TV channels and many others are planned. These channels present talk shows and religious programs, among others which are both educational and entertaining. International TV channels such as National Geographic and History channels, and news channels such as Al Jazeera are well received among Muslims. The BBC, EuroNews, Bloomberg and the CNN are also among the choices, albeit with reservations. International sports channels remain favourites for young Muslims. Finally, children's channels such Arabic Spacetoon, Toyor Aljannah and Karameesh are gaining an increased popularity among Muslim children.

11. Status check. Couples checking in have to provide documents to prove they are married.

12. In-house religious figures that host seminars and preaching sessions. In addition to seminars and preaching those figures are indispensible in the life of Muslims; they answer questions and provide guidance to Muslims and enable them to know the ruling of their religion on issues where they seek enlightenment, which spans all areas of the life of a Muslim, whether business, family, or individual.

13. Art should not depict the human form.

14. Traditional uniforms. The key point here is that the dress should fulfil the three conditions of an Islamic dress; it shouldn't be short, tight or revealing in any way. Traditional uniforms fulfil these

conditions and evoke a sort of nostalgia, a passion for the past, a beautiful yet unattainable state of being.

15.   Beds are not to be placed in the direction of Mecca. A Muslim sleeps on his right side with face towards Mecca, left hand extended along the body, and right hand placed under the cheek. The location of the hotel will determine the direction of the bed. For example, a bed in a hotel in New York, US, means that the person faces east with head south and legs extended north, while a person in China will face west with head north and legs south; it all depends on the exact location of the hotel in relation to Mecca.

16.   Toilets must not be facing Mecca. Like the position of beds above, this is not a matter of *Halal* or *Haram*; it is a matter of showing respect to Islam's holiest place.

17.   Quran, prayer mats, subha (prayer beads) in each room or at the front desk. Many Western hotels provide bibles in guests' rooms. In an Islamic hotel, Islamic materials are provided instead.

Although some of these points represent core services without which a hotel cannot be classified as Islamic, many of them make up the augmented Islamic hospitality experience needed to compete in this emerging field where competition is being based more and more, not on the core *Halal* attributes offered at the Islamic hotel, but on the finer touches that are seen as Islamic but are not usually classified as *Halal* or *Haram*.

Special Challenges Facing Islamic Hospitality

1.   Couples who are not married. Asking non-married couples checking in to provide documents to prove they are married is a sensitive issue that needs to be approached with care. Islam's view on extramarital relations is unswerving; it is forbidden and condemned as one of the major sins. The fact that the policy of an Islamic hotel allows only singles and families should be made clear beforehand in order to avoid embarrassment at check-in and to spare unaware guests the trouble of trying to find an alternative hotel. Unsuspecting guests who arrive at check-in should be turned down gently and helped to find alternative accommodation. One

point need to be iterated here is that some self-proclaimed Islamic hotels tend to be flexible.

2.   Music. Islamic hotels do not play traditional music; there is no rock and roll, no rap, no blues and no Mozart! Moreover, since most non-Muslims wouldn't be familiar with Islamic music and it will be difficult to teach them about it during their short stays, Islamic hotels need to provide alternative entertainment, both private in room entertainment and public in the hotel in general. Giving guests the opportunity to meet each other, if they so wish, through common activities that are open for all to participate will allow guests to entertain as well as give them a chance to network.

3.   Flexibility over certain matters. One point that needs to be iterated here is that some of the self-proclaimed Islamic hotels tend to be 'flexible' in dealing with some of the issue they face. The regional director of marketing at a four-star Dubai hotel in Dubai explains: 'Sometimes we are faced with cases where non-Arab couples arrive and they are not married. We find it rude to turn them away, so we can be a bit flexible with new arrivals and let them stay in the same room, just as long as they behave.' The hotel though does not explain what is and what is not acceptable behaviour, knowing that unmarried couples are not allowed to mix in public, but nevertheless sleep in the same room. A reason underlying this unwarranted flexibility might lie in the fact that 'many companies choose to open Islamic hotels, not for any ethical reason but because they are becoming profitable'. Hotel owners and managers need to know that where there is a clear Islamic principle on a matter there is no room for flexibility or second interpretations. Even flexibility has its limits.

4.   Unqualified staff. Islamic hotels are facing the same problem that Islamic banks have been having since they were first established in the 1970s; qualified employees are in short supply. So far there are no Islamic hospitality degrees and education in this field continues to be carried out on ad hoc bases. As a result hotels tend to apply only Muslims and assume that, because they are Muslims, they know how to behave Islamically, a wrong assumption indeed since Muslims have only lately have remembered the teaching of their Prophet: 'And your smile in the face of your brother is a charity'.

Training, which could be expensive even for Muslim staff , needs to be carried out professionally either in house or outside, although it is also hard to find qualified trainers in this emerging field to train enough people to fill all the vacancies.

5.   Loss of revenue from the sale of alcohol. A major challenge to building and running an Islamic hotel is the loss of revenue from selling alcohol, which contributes about five per cent of a hotel's revenue in a traditional Western-style hotel. Because hotels in the region are social hubs, many people frequent the hotel not to stay but to socialize and return home at the end of the night, the alcohol contribution could be even higher in the region than its counterparts in the West. For an Islamic hotel this type of customers will most likely be lost. Therefore, without revenue from alcohol, Islamic hotels need to generate new and creative revenue streams and strive for higher occupancy.

6.   Marketing. Are these hotels dry hotels or Islamic hotels? Do they position themselves as 'Islamic'? If they were branded as Islamic, would that alienate the non-Muslim clientele? Since most non-Muslim customers will not be aware of all the benefits that Islamic hotels offer, Islamic hoteliers need to educate the market and the consumers in order to create awareness about what Islamic hotels are, how they operate and how are they different from other hotels.

Conclusion

Without alcohol, night clubs, open gender mixing and Western music, the Islamic hotel experience might not be for everyone. Nonetheless, those who are interested in them are enough to keep this sector of hospitality going for a long time before it reaches maturity; it is rapidly growing and planned to capture 10 per cent of the US$1 trillion to be invested in hotels in the Middle East by 2020. Shariah-compliant hotels, where most investment in Islamic hospitality is directed, have only recently begun to spread, although dry hotels, which are commonly confused with Islamic hotels, have for many years existed in Saudi Arabia, Qatar and Kuwait out of necessity. Since alcohol in these countries is prohibited, hotels were wrongly classified as Islamic, which created serious branding and positioning problems. While hoteliers knew that operating dry hotels is represents an attraction to some, as much as it is detested by others, they also recognized that relying on being dry is not enough to create a distinguishable hotel identity that can differentiate the hotel from others. Without such a clear identity a dry hotel is just another hotel that is missing a key ingredient in the hotel business: alcohol. And who needs a 'dry' hotel at the outskirts of the Empty Quarter?

Since Arab travellers and holiday goers will continue to represent a very large portion of this sector's patrons for the foreseeable future, and since in the Arabic consciousness there are very few words that are as detested as much as the word 'dry', *nashif or jaaf* in the Arabic language, hotels in the region certainly need a different way of branding themselves. Being dry, in other words not serving alcohol, and the abstract meaning and associations the word 'dry' attracts, are not selling points in today's approach to this emerging type of hospitality. While the word 'dry' has certain connotations in the Western culture in general, it doesn't yield the same within Arabic and Islamic culture. Arab travellers look for oases to escape to and that is how hotels targeting them should be branded.

Key Terms:

- Dry hotels
- Islamic hotels
- Islamic hospitality
- Arab hospitality
- Religious tourism
- Muslim traveller
- Islamic lifestyles
- Islamic hotel branding
- Islamic hotel identity.

References

Al-Hamarneh, A. and C. Steiner (2004). 'Islamic tourism: rethinking the strategies of tourism development in the Arab world after September 11, 2001.' *Comparative Studies of South Asia, Africa and the Middle East* 24(1): 18–27.

Bakr, A. (2008). 'Islamic hotels have room for growth.' *The National*. 23 April, p. 8

Din, K. H. (1989). 'Islam and tourism: patterns, issues and options.' *Annals of Tourism Research* 16: 542–63.

EZsoftech. (n.d.). 'Islam and generosity (Sakhawat): The power of giving.' Retrieved 23 August 2010, from http://www.ezsoftech.com/stories/mis15.asp.

Jaffery, R. (2009). 'Entertainment in Islam – impossible?' *Islamic Insights*, 17 September. Retrieved 24 August 2010, from http://www.islamicinsights.com/religion/religion/entertainment-in-islam-%E2%80%93-impossible.html.

Javed, N. (2007). 'Islamic hotel branding & Muslim hospitality.' *DinarStandard*, 20 September. Retrieved 25 January 2010, from http://www.dinarstandard.com/marketing/MuslimHospitality092007.htm.

Nomani, M. M. (n.d.). 'Good manners and noble qualities.' *al-islam.edu.pk*. Retrieved 23 August 2010, from http://www.al-islam.edu.pk/whatisislam/goodmaner.htm.

Stephenson, M. L., K. A. Russell, et al. (2010). 'Islamic hospitality in the UAE: indigenization of products and human capital.' *Journal of Islamic Marketing* 1(1): 9–24.

Thomas, K. (2008). 'Islamic hospitality sector emerges.' *MEED: Middle East Economic Digest* 52(18): 55–7.

Index

If you have found this book useful you may be interested in other titles from Gower

Competitive Intelligence
Gathering, Analysing and Putting it to Work
Christopher Murphy
Hardback: 978-0-566-08537-6
e-book: 978-0-7546-8287-5

Brand Risk
Adding Risk Literacy to Brand Management
David Abrahams
Hardback: 978-0-566-08724-0
e-book: 978-0-7546-8890-7

Gender, Design and Marketing
How Gender Drives our Perception of Design and Marketing
Gloria Moss
Hardback: 978-0-566-08786-8

Memorable Customer Experiences
Edited by
Adam Lindgreen, Joëlle Vanhamme and Michael B. Beverland
Hardback: 978-0-566-08868-1
e-book: 978-0-566-09207-7

GOWER

The Psychology of Marketing
Cross-Cultural Perspectives
Gerhard Raab, G. Jason Goddard, Riad A. Ajami and Alexander Unger
Hardback: 978-0-566-08903-9
e-book: 978-0-566-08904-6

Shopping 3.0
Shopping, the Internet or Both?
Cor Molenaar
Hardback: 978-1-4094-1764-4
e-book: 978-1-4094-1765-1

Visit **www.gowerpublishing.com** and

- search the entire catalogue of Gower books in print
- order titles online at 10% discount
- take advantage of special offers
- sign up for our monthly e-mail update service
- download free sample chapters from all recent titles
- download or order our catalogue